LEGLESS MAN IN TOPLESS BAR

LEGLESS MAN IN TOPLESS BAR

THE SOME OF
PAUL HAMILTON

Bracketpress × Actually Pretty Ltd.

Published by Bracketpress
in conjunction with Actually Pretty Ltd.,
Littleborough OL15 9EL England

Cover photograph by Alice Smith
Typesetting by Christian Brett

Printed and bound by
TJ Books Ltd.
Padstow PL28 8RW

ISBN 978-1-7393290-3-7

Dedicated to

Linda Guilding
(Drama teacher, The Vyne School, Basingstoke, 1975–1980)

and

Anna Hills
(Drama teacher, Basingstoke Technical College, 1980–1982)

who will most probably never see,
or know of, this book.

CONTENTS

"Come *on*, then..."

Herein is *not*, you'll be relieved to learn, poetry. Rather, this is a selection of words written for the sole intention of being warbled, yodelled, crooned or yelled over musical accompaniment. This is not a definitive collection of all the *Complete Works* as be-quilled by my cig-gripping, nail-gnawed paws while I was ravin' over a writing desk. No, this is a pick of songwords that, despite being torn out from their audio-toriums, may still amuse in this paper view context. Unlike poetry, songwords are better said than read, so feel free to bellow, declaim or grumble this miscellany wherever you find yourself – a rush-hour train, a council meeting, a library, a hospital operating theatre, a church (very good for echo), during a forehead-clenching critical moment of a snooker championship final – till your heart's content.

Despite protests to the contrary propounded by pompous panjandrums, pop song lyrics are never poetry. Yer rock'n'rolling songwriter has neither the time nor energy to maintain the consistency or discipline of the poetic form. A song's structure can be likened to a joke in that, over the space of a couple of minutes, the scene must be established with its protagonists swiftly but effectively drawn. Then there must be action, a scenario, the element of drama, a conflict, an argument resulting – before the last reprise of the chorus – in a punchline to resolve or conclude the story.

It has been my good fortune to play with some inspiring, inventive musicians and champion chums. I hope I raised their game as much as they raised mine. This indulgence of a book is dedicated to my musical muckers who have weaved in and out of my forty year tapestry of tapes:
Simon Beacon
Doug Murphy
Dave Pope
Andy Thomson

It is they who are my mind's audience when I write songwords. Inventing rhymes for one's own amusement is valid, up to a point, but it is their delight and joy when they are tickled by a particular line that makes everything worthwhile.

And winding the tape back to its beginning, there's Gary Page (*a.k.a.* Harry Flames, Lascivious Cage, X-Devious Rage, Larry Strange, Lionel Beige and a zillion other derivations) with his brother's two-string guitar which Flames had decorated with the hand-painted legend "This GIT-argh kills music" – perhaps unknowingly channelling Woody Guthrie's guitar-slogan "This machine kills fascists" – sitting on the edge of my bed in November 1978. Between him and me (sitting on the floor before a crescent of saucepans, buckets and spoons) was a tape recorder. The reason for our collating this clutter about us was because I had read an interview in *Melody Maker* where Pink Floyd keyboardist Rick Wright said that his group had begun recording a new concept album that would probably take a year to complete. "A year to make a record?" I scoffed:

"Lazy sods. We could make one in an afternoon."
Flames rose to the challenge with, "Come *on*, then..."

Needless to say, our hugger-mugger effort - some 40 minutes of twanging, banging and haranguing - was caterwauling drivel, free from the oppressive strictures of rhythm, melody and harmony, but the seeds were sown.

Most of the songwords gathered here are self-explanatory. One needn't ponder whether one particular selection contains a knowing reference to some dusty poem or if another is a withering satirical barb attacking some time-locked political outrage, because they're almost entirely not. True, *Invitation To A Beheading* shares the same title as a Vladimir Nabokov novel, but I've never read it; I simply saw the title and used it as a starting point for a song. *Kolibri* is probably the only item based on historical fact, "Kolibri" (or "hummingbird") being the codeword for the instigation of The Night Of The Long Knives (June 30th–July 2nd, 1934). The last verse fast-forwards to the execution of Troy Davis by lethal injection on September 21st, 2011. *Best* is a fantasia about the footballing legend George Best.

Very little of my peachfluff-chinned, shagspot-faced adolescent efforts are included. This is because they are, for the most part, unbearable drivel; 'apprenticeship' songs would be a kinder description, learning the trade. Only *Puke Bloooz* has crept in as it is perhaps the least toe-curling and possesses the faintest trace of merit. Well, it still makes me laugh, anyway.

There is also a paucity of examples from the mid-1980s. Despite being the principal co-writer (with Dave Pope) for the art school tosser group Horrible Head, I find much of our material, although transferred from paper to the stage with a modicum of success, doesn't make the journey back to the page satisfactorily. *Black And White Lines*, *I'm A Loser*, *Pretend* and *They Don't Need Me*, despite a sepia tinge, retain some attraction. *Not Your Property* suffered from a wilful vagueness which I addressed in 2012. *This Is All You Get* was the first collaboration with Pope. It was originally a list of subjects I wanted to paint written down in a sketchbook. (We were, as mentioned a few sentences back, both art students.) He saw this series of topics and up-piped, "That could make a song!" And so it did. Apart from the chorus, the content is pretty much the original list with very little alteration or embellishment.

In the 1990s, I was rudderless and drifting without a musical ensemble to steer me. [*That's enough nautical metaphors, you weigh-anchor. – Ed.*] Despite this setback, I continued writing songwords but, for the most part, they were piffle, waffle, fluff, stuff and nonsense. Realising their worthlessness, I stopped the practise in 1995 and didn't resume until a decade later. The only diamonds in the dungheap were *Moon Rising Over London* (which was recorded by three different groups in three different arrangements) and *These Shoes* (also interpreted on three separate occasions). The selections share a certain unhappiness in the subject matter but my sincere wish is that the reader will find some uplifting element amongst all the torment and tears.

The remainder of this volume is from 2005 to 2023. Practically everything included here has been recorded but one needn't seek out the singles, EPs and albums to attain a fuller, deeper understanding of what is going on or being said. They are as plain, or as pretty, or as bulbous and veiny, as the nose on your face. Whereas songs can benefit from the repetition of choruses (and, occasionally, verses), they can suffer when transposed to the page; therefore, many of the choruses have been blue-pencilled to prevent eye-stabbing boredom setting in. The selections have been set out in an alphabetical rather than chronological order. This is because there is no true 'development' or 'progression' in my writing. Every time, for me, is the first time - although, I find, with each successive song having been written, there's always the feeling that I've run out of subjects to write about and ways in which to say something. Perhaps I have only dealt with one subject all this time, and used only one approach and a single, unchanging style. Well, that is for you to discover to your delight or dismay.

The songwords await you at the turn of a page. Well, come *on*, then!

Paul Hamilton
London, 11:34am 22 July 2024.

168

Ticket number 156
Please go to counter 7
Ticket number 157
Please go to counter 4
Ticket number 158
Please go to counter 1
Ticket number 159
Please go to counter 5
Ticket number 160
Please go to counter 12
Ticket number 161
Please go to counter 3
Ticket number 162
Please go to counter 11
Ticket number 163
Please go to counter 2

I am number 168
How much longer must I wait?
How much longer must I wait?

Ticket number 164
Please go to counter 8
Ticket number 165
Please go to counter 10
Ticket number 166
Please go to counter 6
Ticket number 167
Please go to counter 9

Ticket number 167
        Please go to counter 9
Ticket number 167
        Please go to counter 9
Ticket number 169
        Please go to counter 7
Ticket number 170
        Please go to counter 4

I am number 168
How much longer must I wait?
How much longer must I wait?

Ticket number 171
        Please go to counter 11
Ticket number 172
        Please go to counter 7
Ticket number 173
        Please go to counter 2
Ticket number 174
        Please go to counter 1...

A KARAOKE VERSION OF MYSELF

I'm empty as a condemned flat,
I'm disconnected and cold.
You get emotional, I get my hat,
The sign on my soul says 'Sold'.
I maybe flogged it to the Devil in a Faustian pact
In exchange for sex and fame and wealth.
I've seen little of that
But it's a transparent fact
I'm a karaoke version of myself.

She stopped being the person I fell in love with,
I never became what she wanted me to be.
And when she left I found I lost the gift to give;
I'm paying the price for being free.
I'll be with the legless men in a topless bar,
Get wrecked wishing ourselves "Good health!"
I'm in the queue of goons,
Await my turn to croon tunes:
I'm a karaoke version of myself.

There are visions of beauty that can make a heart melt;
Mine will neither thaw or bend.
I take drugs to remember to drink to forget
Situations I can't wreck or mend.
I sidestep sorrow, misery misses by miles,
I'm out to lunch should you call for help.
These tears are pure crocodile,
I use coat-hangers to smile:
I'm a karaoke version of myself.

I've extinguished the fires,
Cut all the wires—
Karaoke version of myself.

My heart is a fridge.
Is this the verse or the bridge?
I just do these lines,
There's no reason in rhyme.
Here, tonight,
Here, tonight,
Here, tonight
Here, tonight—
A KARAOKE VERSION OF MYSELF!

A MAN FOR ALL TREASONS

If I can avoid every crack in the pavement
And understand what the poems of Verlaine meant,
If I can make five anagrams out of Alice B. Toklas,
If I can keep my white shirt spotless
Then she will appear to me topless.
Then my situation won't be hopeless.
Then she will fall in love with me
But that day will never be—

Unless I see a green car with an L reg plate,
Recite the alphabet backwards with no hesitate—
Shun the unknown paper seller shouting,
    "Wotcha, mate!"
If I keep my hands in my pockets
    when I open the gate
Then she will appear to me, not a second too late
And I'll be spared a life worse than fate
'Cos she will fall in love with me
But that day will never be—

Until I count every railing on Coronation Road,
Recite Derek & Clive's duologue about
    the Barking Toad,
If I know how many times a piece of paper can fold,
If I know how penicillin is derived from mould,
Then she will offer her hand to hold;
I'll be her action man, she'll be my doll.
Then she will fall in love with me
But that day will never be—

Because I didn't catch the first leaf falling from
that tree,
I didn't brush up on rudimentary geometry,
I never translated *War And Peace* into Swahili,
I forgot the name of the hit song by Peters & Lee,
I put my left sock on first instead of my right,
I didn't charge my phone overnight,
I failed to recognise the flags of all nations,
I didn't take my hat off in the underground station
And that is why she
Will never fall in love with me.
And that is why she
Will never fall in love with me.

BABYLON DON

This three colour collar
Cost me a duller dollar.
Stick it on ... Babylon Don.
Win some, lose some,
Grin some, booze some;
This round's on ... Babylon Don.

Babylon Don – reaching his peak,
Babylon Don – he's here all week,
Babylon Don – he's going to speak.
Take it down, take it in;
Brixton Nick knows where he's been.
Now everything's irie, mon
With Babylon Don.

His front: posh, ambitious.
He's back: washing dishes.
Rinse and shine on ... Babylon Don.
Kit for the smirking classes:
Git your leather sunglasses.
Puttin' 'em on... Babylon Don.

Playing dead on the sofa,
Spent bread, a jammy loafer;
He's toast, garçon ... Babylon Don.
By day: a pasty face-ster.
By night: a tasty waster.
Merci, bon ... Babylon Don.

Babylon Don – burning in the shades,
Babylon Don – a blaze of razorblades,
Babylon Don – see white straights fade.
Take it up, take it in,
Smarten out that stupid grin;
Wipe it off and get it on
With Babylon Don.

Sniff that whiff of here-aftershave
Mixed with spliff-smoke rising from his grave
Pass it on ... it's Babylon Don.

BEST

Make way for the dying legend
Living down to expectations;
Out of your league for class and style, and
Deconstructing state relations.

The richest embarrassment of talent,
I'm asked in a tone that mocks,
"Your obsession with sex and soccer –
    is it all about getting a tackle in the box?"

In your hero top ten I'm first
And even at my very worst
I'm Best!
I'm Best!
    Best! Looking great in shorts and vest
    Best! The ladies love my hairy chest
    Scoring for the boring, playing the field
    All angles covered, unnaturally skilled
I'm Best!

Have my pills swallowed themselves?
Did my bed grow that English rose there?
And has my vodka drunk itself?
It was all there last night, I swear!

What tailor embroidered sick on my suit?
Have my cigarettes smoked themselves right down?
I've thrown away my kingdom
But I've still got half a crown

You may spot me sporting a poultice
And here's another thing you can't fail to notice
I'm Best!
I'm Best!
    Best! Looking great in shorts and vest
    Best! The ladies love my hairy chest
    Blarney stone swallower, playing the field
    All angles covered, unnaturally skilled
I'm Best!
Yeah yeah yeah - I'm Best!

There's always a backslapper wants to buy me
    a drink
And all of his friends, they've got to buy me a drink
Till my grin is fixed and down I sink
Sink into the ditches.
That's when those sons of bitches
Start taking all their pictures:
Flash! flash! flash! snap those jokers
But even though I'm out of focus

I'm Best!
I'm Best!
    Best! Looking great in shorts and vest
    Best! The ladies love my hairy chest
    Best! Grandstanding, playing the field
    Best! All angles covered, unnaturally skilled
I'm Best!

I do solemnly confess
I'm Best!
    Check the family crest
I'm Best!
    Yes! yes! yes!
I'm Best!

BEYOND

Beyond the mind that held the thought
Beyond the skull that holds the brain
Beyond the eyes that shape the face
And shape the world for mind to see
Beyond this room and all it holds
Beyond you there, you read, you drink,
Beyond open nightgown, invite
Me in again, ha ha, oh yes
Beyond daylight flooding indoors
Rooftops rain-wet, the cloud rolls by
Beyond the planes silent and small,
Their trails like lace that tie the world
Within our reach but still so long
Beyond the sky, the moon, the sun,
Beyond the edge and end of all
Beyond this time there is nothing.

There is nothing, nothing at all.

BILL'S BRILL GRILL

"Mushroom, sausage, eggs, beans, toast twice,
Scrambled egg, cup of gnat's and a fried slice."

Slight variations on the above
Completed with a "Cheers, darlin'" or "Thanks, love"
Are pretty much all that's ever said to me
A woman manning the till of Bill's Brill Grill nosherie.

Oldie radio station's doing in my head
I only took on this job to pay off my debts
The one thing money can't buy is poverty
Underpaid, under the cosh in
    Bill's Brill Grill nosherie.

"Mushroom, sausage, eggs, beans, toast twice,
Scrambled egg, cup of gnat's and a fried slice."

A steady stream of hard hats from the building site
Gold-toothed grins and "Hey, wotcher doin' tonight?"
Play your cards right and you could be doing me
Banging my bored brains out in
    Bill's Brill Grill nosherie.

One day a gold limo will screech in the street
And in will stride a zillionaire who'll sweep me off
    my feet
Jet me off to his mansion in Los Angeles
Rolling in dosh far away from
    Bill's Brill Grill nosherie.

“Mushroom, sausage, eggs, beans, toast twice,
Scrambled egg, cup of gnat’s and a fried slice.
Mushroom, sausage, eggs, beans, toast twice,
Scrambled egg, cup of gnat’s and a fried slice.”

BLACK AND WHITE LINES

Showbiz politicians' unslapped wrists
Operate the undercover torture twists.
In a two-minute spot we barely get the gist
Because Dad's shouting between mouthfuls
    of crisps.
Just sit at the table and eat your tea
There's no brain-food on prime-time TV.

Wailing widows in familiar foreign rubble
Whining dogs limping away from trouble
Talking heads and camera crews zoom in on
    the bereaved
Solemnly sloganizing their facts we should believe.
Just do as you're told and eat your tea
There's no brain-food on prime-time TV.

And if it gets too much
It only takes a touch
And we can turn over and go to sleep.
It's only black and white lines on a twelve-inch
    screen,
With the remote control we can eliminate the
    screams
And dream...
And dream...

Oh, you're so good at taking the piss –
"Come in here and get a load of this!"

You think it's so awfully funny
'Cos it ain't YOU and it's so far away.
Just take your orders and eat your tea,
These are your faves on prime-time TV.

And if it gets too real
And you feel a strange chill,
You can turn over and fall asleep.
It's only black and white lines on a twelve-inch
    screen.
With a push of a button you can kill reality
And dream...
    AND DREAM AND DREAM AND DREAM!
It's only black and white lines on a twelve-inch
    screen
And what they're saying,
    you don't care what it means.
You feel so safe 'cos you've got nothing to believe
And a push of a button can kill reality.

BLAND FOUNDATION

I am Locus Operative 4CB
Personnel correlator level 2/3
Tooth-tapping pen-chewing countdown to pension
Handsome pay-off from The Bland Foundation

THIS IS THE BLAND FOUNDATION,
        THE BLAND FOUNDATION
Turning sloppy seconds into uniform years
THIS IS THE BLAND FOUNDATION,
        THE BLAND FOUNDATION
Direct inject blancmange in your ears

The Impersonal Adipose Tissue Net Effect
Propose International Health
    then go and get wrecked
The fizzy cool jerks, mental masturbation
There lies the rub with The Bland Foundation

THIS IS THE BLAND FOUNDATION,
        THE BLAND FOUNDATION
Bang the dole drums soft and scary
THIS IS THE BLAND FOUNDATION,
        THE BLAND FOUNDATION
Making life extra-ordinary

We're fascinated by your every opinion
Fill in these forms, collected by a minion
Under-managers Friday drink with tidy Jeff
Pray you're not replaced by a Slavetron VAF

BY THE BLAND FOUNDATION,
THE BLAND FOUNDATION
Nigel Havers supplies website narration
THE BLAND FOUNDATION,
THE BLAND FOUNDATION
Thank God you're not Malaysian

Looking for danger, security, car, prospects,
Loud tie, quiet life, dead wife, office sex
Perfect company, the right occasion
Perfect fitting golden handcuffs –
THE BLAND FOUNDATION

THIS IS THE BLAND FOUNDATION,
THE BLAND FOUNDATION
Use the news, lose the old
THIS IS THE BLAND FOUNDATION,
THE BLAND FOUNDATION
All that glitters turns to mould

BLUEBELL WOOD

Do they still call this Bluebell Wood
Where ne'er-do-wells did no good?
Hit by lit darts fired by the sun
Travelling like javelins shot from God's gun

Where dens, hide-outs and secret magic palaces
Backed on to the fenced,
      immense garden of the Harrises.

Life was a song and laughter its tune,
The world was a pudding, I was a spoon.
It seemed bigger in my wild childhood.
Do they still call this Bluebell Wood?

Do they still call this Shady Glade
Where bogeymen would stalk and we'd be afraid?
Camp fire cramped, frying pan and kettle
Bangers and beans, dock leaves and nettles,

Talk of Chinese burns, Scotch mist,
      what a French kiss is
As a damp burning branch crackles and hisses.

Barry boasts he drank a Martini
Then was sick on his dad's Lamborghini
Barry? Or was it Gary? Memories fade...
Do they still call this Shady Glade?

Do they still call this Bluebell Wood?
Did we jam roly-poly home for roast dins and pud?
We would meet when shadows were short,
Hold up the jars of prisoners we'd caught.

Tadpoles, earwigs, daddy longlegs, worms;
Capture a lizard, you're a wizard of the firm.

This was back when a box had three sides
And pennies got a multitude of chews and rides
And two years in the Army would do you good.
Do they still call this Bluebell Wood?

BORN TO REST

I have to stop for a lay-down
While taking forty winks.
Jimmy-jams are my uniform
My eyelids are on the blink.
Not a bead of sweat on my forehead
Never a sinew flexed.
General Strike, I salute you
Major Breakdown, you're next.

I could've been a long distance runner
But I'm always short of breath
I could have been a gung-ho soldier
But I'm allergic to death.
I'd give a sloth a walk for his money
I've got slo-mo beat
Instant coma's gonna get me
I need speed to sleep.

University of Loaf? I never took the test
No winning tape touched my breast
I'm too beat to beat my chest
Baby, I was born to rest.

Swimming across the channel
Is an ambition successfully ducked.
I could have been a high-class gigolo
But I couldn't be fucked.

Tune out, drop off, be someone else's guest
Beware the Jabberwock, Sudoko and incest
Three zeds are my family crest
Baby, I was born to rest.

BREAKFAST OF CHAMPIONS

The breakfast of champions today
Fails to mask the bitter taste
Punchlines mistimed, affections misplaced
Loss of cool, loss of nerve, loss of face.
Rewrite last night with a nine-hand shake
Loathe it or hate it,
    that's the choice you've got to make.
Where's the glitter in the gutter,
    the gloomer of glam?
It's taken me an eternity to understand
'Nothing lasts forever' – POW! BAM!
Count your friends on the toes of one hand
Spray paint your achievements on a grain of sand
Collapse into a chaos meticulously planned
Like the breakfast of champions,
    your audience's laughter is canned.

Street party Mardi Gras; you didn't get an invite
They smile and see you out; lie, "It's an oversight"
It *ssssssssssssucks* but you don't bite
Your mouth's too loose when you're too tight.
They turn you out, turn away and turn off the light
And you fold into the shadows of the night.
You're the bad mood parachute
    crashing down their good time venue
But the breakfast of champions remains your menu.

I used to drop names but, one by one,
    the names dropped me
In the glass and steel jungle
    I'm at the top of the soli-tree
My portrait will never hang in the In Vogue Gallery
I want to go home, wherever that may be
That may be.

BRITISH EMPIRE STATE

Was it the baba ghanoush
On the rare Scotch blackface
That triggered my rainbow of vomit?
I gargle mouthwash
Throw on a fresh shirt
Hit the bar for gin and catatonic.

A perspiring Frenchman
Here on business
Like the natives, asks if I'm American;
I flash a row of pearlies
"Nottingham in England;
I'm the middle-born of five privileged sons."

He's in export –
Gorilla hand ashtrays,
Elephant foot umbrella stands;
I check my gold Hunter
Make my excuses
And mingle 'neath the fly-carousel ceiling fans.

Is it the crap tobacco
Or the horse piss vino
That perfumes the air with halitosis?
I can't stand it here
And I can't stand here
This jet-lagger's got executive class of thrombosis.

One more day
Then I'm gone - mañana.
Bloodshot eyes glazed
From the smoke of Havanas;
I'm trying to remain
In a British Empire state.
I have to stay and wait
For a certain date.

I see a figure rush
I feel my hand crushed
"Name's Walters, seconded from the old firm."
Finger click; a tray of gins
Fills me up and he fills me in:
"Keep it under your hat, not a murmur."

We leave the sex tourists,
Hail and board a rickshaw,
The buildings puke out pavements of workers.
Proceeding at a steady jog,
Walters bangs out a monologue:
"You can only trust Yorkshiremen and Gurkhas."

False passport, currency,
Duplicate hotel key:
"He'll be back before midnight so let's go."
Destination reached,
I step out on the street;
He rides off into the clouds of teargas and discos.

Midnight comes and goes,
The target doesn't show.
4am I'm half-asleep, leaning on the balustrade.
Explosion rips my shirt and vest,
Blood pumps out my chest.
Walters there, with a gun and gorilla hand ashtray.

One more day
Now I'm gone - adios, mañana.
Bloodshot eyes glazed
Bulging like an iguana's.
I'm lying on the carpet
In a British Empire state.
I have to stay and wait
For a certain date.

CARRIER BAGS

Saw St. Christopher on the night bus
He said he's going home;
"Can't do nothing for you, son," he said,
"From now on you're on your own."

No walls reach my ceiling,
No rugs touch my floor,
The sun is a mouldy corn plaster,
The moon's a blistered sore.

My veins are stuffed with dust and fluff,
Cobwebs and teabags,
(Tramp tramp tramp!)
My brains are drained of notions and potions,
I measure my life in fags
(Tramp tramp!)
And the weight of my carrier bags.

The lamp posts are bending over,
They're listening to what I say.
Eyeballs in every letter box
Watching, hoping I walk away.

I'm in-between womb and tombstone,
Am I thirty or seventy-three?
Don't lose your marbles when I quit the game
Name a sandwich after me.

"One gathers he owns a string of race horses."
"I heard he was in on the Hatton Garden sparklers
blag."
"I heard he was the ninth Beatle."
"Ah, I'm afraid I haven't heard anything at all!"

My veins are stuffed with dust and fluff,
Cobwebs and teabags,
(Tramp tramp tramp!)
My brains are drained of notions and potions,
I measure my life in fags
(Tramp tramp!)
And the weight of my carrier bags.
And the weight of my carrier bags.

COTTAGE BY THE SEA

To be
In a cottage by the sea;
Happy
That's the dream for you and me.
Fruit tree
And cricket on the BBC.
A glorious boundary
Around our cottage by the sea.

Belts kept tightened
Never daring to eat,
Freezing all winter
Shivering under one sheet.
Every penny we earned
We had to hoard it
To buy our dream home;
Now we can afford it.

A little white cottage
On the golden coast.
Sunday morning aroma
Boiled eggs, tea and toast.
Hand-carved wooden nameplate
Beside the unlocked front door.
A leisurely stroll or bike ride
To the village store.

To be
In a cottage by the sea;
Happy
That's the dream for you and me.
Fruit tree
And the last remaining bee
Busy busy, unlike you and me
In our cottage by the sea.

I'll build a greenhouse
For me to sit in
To smoke my fags while
You do your knitting.
Write our kids long letters,
They send us postcards
Saying they can't visit:
Selfish bastards.

To be
In a cottage by the sea;
Happy
That's the end for you and me.
Agree
Life's not what it used to be.
Thank God
For our cottage by the sea.

DEAD LEG

Dead leg – it's the living end
Dead leg – I'm twisted, going round the bend
Dead leg – don't be a fool, it's a bad trip
These are the days my diary dearly wants to skip
Dead leg...

I'm confined to this scratchy bed,
Doctor's orders I must obey,
With a divebombing fly for company,
Like a toppled dictator's statue I lay
    Watching shadows grow.
    Where does the wind go?
    Praise Marx and pass the laudanum.
    If I don't get well soon,
    Next stop: autopsy room.
    Cause of death: overdose of boredom.

Left foot painfully elevated,
A horizontal stormtrooper.
My unpillowed bean can't see the TV,
Steaming in a semi-super stupor.
    The control
    It's too remote;
    It's inches beyond my clawing reach.
    And where's my wallet?
    Nurse has got it!
    Melting my cards on some scorching beach...
Dead leg – it's the living end
Dead leg – I'm twisted, going round the bend

For all the social sympathedia
And smiley-faced wishes for a cure-all,
My guest book remains unsigned,
It's just two names away from going plural.
    This is how
    I realise now
    Why my bedside is people-nude here.
    Social media, aye?
    Is one fat stinking lie;
    What they mean is social you, dear.

Bananas are bruised, all the water's used,
Batteries and fags have run out.
Could this so-called life get any wronger?
Of course it can! Come in, Mr Gout
Oh, that's torn it –
    There's a thousand hornets
    Drilling their way out of my big toe.
    Their over-sharpened picks
    Are sulphuric acid-tipped;
    They've hit a nerve and they won't let go.

Dead leg – it's the living end
Dead leg – I'm twisted, going round the bend
Dead leg – don't be a fool, it's a bad trip
These are the days my diary dearly wants to skip
Dead leg

DO IT MYSELF

The ceiling inspector's coming
No time to relax
Got to check for dampness
Got to fill in the cracks
Pass me the lubricant
This joint's very stiff
Give me a bunk-up
We'll have it off in a jiff.

Despite the fruit and fibre
A man of my calibre
Must consider his state of health.
So shorten your distance
I need your assistance
I can't do it myself.

It's gonna get messy
So put down some sheets
This job could take hours
I had one that took weeks.
Is the spirit level?
Any oil in the can?
Squeeze it very tightly
It'll come off in your hand.

Despite the fruit and fibre
A man of my calibre
Must consider his state of health.

So get off the sofa
Don't be a crusty loafer
I can't do it myself.

I've whitewashed your back doors
Plastered the hall
I've coated the kitchen
Screwed in a false wall.
You say all this banging
Has gotten you aroused
Do you expect me to do you
After I've done up the house?

Despite the fruit and fibre
A man of my calibre
Must consider his state of health.
I'll get out my tools
You get out your overalls
I can't do it myself.

DRINKING WITH JESUS

I've been drinking with Jesus
In a bar full of New Cross geezers.
Won the jackpot on the one-armed bandit
Scooping the loot he smiled, "That's the way Dad
    planned it."
I asked him for another miracle;
"O ye of little faith," he said, "don't get cynical"
And made his excuses to go and turn wine
Into urine.

I've been drinking with Jesus;
Frayed shirt cuffs, trousers in creases.
Told me of his day trip to the coast
Treating deckchair society to sardines on toast.
"It ain't easy being a famous father's son;
Patricide is tempting but what's the use of a gun
When your target is invisible, immortal?
Unbelievable!"

I've been drinking with Jesus;
Crow's feet, hair like Caesar's.
Looks unlike the man nailed to a crucifix
In churches and round the necks of teenage chicks.
Yesterday's terrorist is tomorrow's freedom fighter;
Like to bring on a friend of us all,
    Mr Nelson Mandela.
He learnt the hard way the average human
Is inhuman.

I've been drinking with Jesus;
Snakebite and blacks, Bicardi Breezers.
Looking away he says he feels hopeless shame
For what maniacs commit in his name.
Taking a backseat, he lets things take their course:
"Let fundamentalists crash the pearly gates by force;
They're not gonna like their heavenly reward:
A sword."

I've been drinking with Jesus.
We're simpatico; I cough, he sneezes.
He sighed, "Although the Vatican's happy to own me,
The sorry truth is the world has outgrown me."
Putting on his coat, he said, "There's no love where
there's doubt."
He turned and waved goodbye. On his way out
I looked at the holes in his hands and I saw the light
And cried.

EVERYONE LIKES THIS

Bitch of betrayal, your squandered vote,
Plagiarise the wise for your status quote.
Advertise a device promising instant bliss;
Everyone likes this.

Repeat the latest joke, guaranteed greatest laughs
On your Blackberry in Macky D, support veal calves.
Heart the bleeding obvious, a hit, you'll never miss;
Everyone likes this.

This is your stage, so sing and dance in Lalaland.
Be the early Beatles, not late Hancock or Garland.
What goes online stays online,
    and there's no escaping.
Your group hug feels like a gang-bang raping.

Don't come here looking for sympathy;
You'll only find it in a dictionary
In between shit and syphilis.
Everyone's like this.

EXCELLENTÉ PRESIDENTÉ

We fly tonight to Barcelona
Bromide pills to soften the boner.
Glide nonchalant through customs
So no green hat barks, "Bust 'em!"
We're sweating, we're nervous,
The lost luggage louts swerve us
We're the gold lamé barmy army;
This town will fold like origami.
We got gas, we got shooters;
In 48 hours generalissimos will salute us.
No slackers, wasters, glassbacks or moaners -
We're taking Barcelona.

We're meticulous 'cos in this game
There's no safety net;
We've studied flamingo dancing
And packed our exploding castanets.

We drive tonight to gay Paree;
Brut 33 is our pot pourri.
There's Jock McHeadlock, ex-Sporran legion;
Ardent Fanny from the leather region.
A mile of fire down the Champs Elysses;
They'll lose their heads if they don't do as we say.
No stopping for a breather;
Our money's in Geneva.
Daily rag - special edition
When we accomplish our mission;

See our capped teeth gleam –
We are the new regime.

Dissenters will hang like christmas balls
From the Eiffel tower.
It's a dirty job but we're cleaning up
Let them eat soap in the shower.

Excellenté, Presidenté!
Welcome to your land of plenty.
Wave to sick and poverty-stricken
From your solid gold car.

We sail tonight into Sydney harbour
Down in Godzone, south of Java.
Screams of "Pommy, can you hear me?"
      in the opera house
Reduced to rubble by Sammy Scouse.
Gonna hack down the eucalyptus trees
Gonna crack down on aborigines;
Send 'em back where they originated.
Liberal intolerance won't be tolerated.
We're cautious, we're nervous
But soon we'll be cruising like kings in our Porsches.
It's a criminal state, a moral failure;
That will change when we take Australia.

Excellenté, Presidenté!
Vile profiles refused entry;
Shots for rabies, you’re kissing babies
From your bulletproof car.

FEATHERSTONEHAUGH, FEATHERSTONEHAUGH, WRIOTHESLEY

They closed down the Ministry of Posterity
Featherstonehaugh, Featherstonehaugh,
  Wriothesley
No future in it, so far as they could see.
Featherstonehaugh, Featherstonehaugh,
  Wriothesley
My move to the Office of Ambiguity
Featherstonehaugh, Featherstonehaugh,
  Wriothesley
Was both accepted and rejected in equal degree.
Featherstonehaugh, Featherstonehaugh,
  Wriothesley

But who won't nose upturn to a snifter?
Turn a blind ear to a blazing bifta?
Won't be miffed by a mental shapeshifter?
Featherstonehaugh, Featherstonehaugh,
  Wriothesley

We got our meathooks in your salad days
Featherstonehaugh, Featherstonehaugh,
  Wriothesley
We coined the phrase "to coin a phrase"
Featherstonehaugh, Featherstonehaugh,
  Wriothesley
We can make cripples crawl amok

Featherstonehaugh, Featherstonehaugh,
    Wriothesley
Blowing our trumpet,
    where there's brass there's muck
Featherstonehaugh, Featherstonehaugh,
    Wriothesley

Slippery shoo-ins get the boot,
Red, white and blue vein in my flute,
Paperclips keep me in suits -
Featherstonehaugh, Featherstonehaugh,
    Wriothesley

Fire a rocket to Accounts, there's a major flap on.
Featherstonehaugh, Featherstonehaugh,
    Wriothesley
The bogs are bugged so turn the tap on.
Featherstonehaugh, Featherstonehaugh,
    Wriothesley
We're the intel plumbers for your security leak,
Featherstonehaugh, Featherstonehaugh,
    Wriothesley
The keep-it-flush-flush boutique clique.
Featherstonehaugh, Featherstonehaugh,
    Wriothesley

We tell you what and who to believe,
You think you've got the Midas disease,

And money to burn in a pay freeze –
Featherstonehaugh, Featherstonehaugh,
    Wriothesley

Christmas beano, mouth oozing froth,
Featherstonehaugh, Featherstonehaugh,
    Wriothesley
Face down in the beef stroganoff,
Featherstonehaugh, Featherstonehaugh,
    Wriothesley
If the CEO sees me he'll be waxing wrath,
Featherstonehaugh, Featherstonehaugh,
    Wriothesley
Saxon, light your farts and set the sprinklers off.
Featherstonehaugh, Featherstonehaugh,
    Wriothesley

I'm Popeyed ODing on nasal spinach;
Crossword puzzles, five mins, finished.
Light in my peepers undiminished -
Featherstonehaugh, Featherstonehaugh,
    Wriothesley

FISHES

Forcing down a second slice of divorce cake
A hand lands on my shoulder and gives me a shake;
I turn and look up to see that it's the big man.
"Son," he says, "there's one thing you must
    understand;
There are plenty more fish in the sea
So stop playing with your tackle or you'll stay lonely."
"Thank you for your advice," I say,
    "you're so kind to give
But let me get things into perspective...

There's a crumb of scum
    stuck between God's toes
    which we call The Universe.
It is comprised of 10,000 superclusters
    each one 100 billion miles long.
And each supercluster contains a 1000 local clusters
    each one 100 million miles long
And each local cluster is divided into
    100 local groups
    each one a million miles long.
Within only one of these local groups
    you'll find the Milky Way.
Within the Milky Way there's the Orion Spur.
Within the Orion Spur is Alpha Centauri,
Adjacent to which is the Solar System.
Inhabiting the Solar System are the superior planets

And amongst them is our planet Earth
    which has a human population of 8 billion,
    50% approximately are female,
Giving me the choice of 4 billion possible partners.
I live in the Northern Hemisphere,
Bringing the number down to 3 billion.
Being in Europe reduces the total to 381 million.
Being in Britain reduces it further to 32 million.
Being in London reduces it to 3 million.
Being south of the river reduces it to 1.5 million.
Being in Brixton reduces it to 20,000.
My being over 40 reduces it to 500.
My looks and personality reduces it further to
    a hundred.
My class and income status whittles it down to ten.
Of this ten I imagine half would be
About as ugly as me
And three would be lesbians,
Leaving one raving Nazi
And the one last remaining one
Who, by process of elimination,
Would be my one true perfect lover
Rests her face on a pillow inside a gas oven
On a quiet Saturday afternoon
And breathes...

Suffocated by the weight of indifference,
Crushed between God's toes,
She found The Universe too small
To find her soul mate.
Well, here I am - and too late.
If only I could have saved her
And she, in turn, saved me
We could have walked along a shoreline
Counting the fishes in the sea
We could've walked the seagull-shadowed shoreline
And watch the fucking fishes."

FOUR CHORDS AND A CAPO

Darling, did you read the letters that
    I left for you to see?
I'm eh-double-you-oh-el, em-eye-ay 'cos
    I can't are-eye-pea.
(He's got four chords and a capo in his case!)
No-one's buying anything, and no-one wants it
    if it's free
But I'm taking egocentric singing lessons:
    "Me, me, me, me, me, me!"
(He's got four chords and a capo in his case!)

Nothing going down in this dead horse town
    but to get stewed and brood;
I'll come back in a platinum yacht full of supermodels
    in the nude.
(He's got four chords and a capo in his case!)
The palace of wisdom looks out on to the road to
    excess
And I'd be a clown not to turn down temptation's
    caress.
(He's got four chords and a capo in his case!)

It's time to punch the air,
    kick some ass and hit the road.
Butt out, strutters;
    obey the My Way Or The Highway Code.
It's a race!
(He's got four chords and a capo in his case!)

Studio booked, riffs and hooks,
    this time I've got it right
With groovy vibes married
    to diatribes of existential plight.
(He's got four chords and a capo in his case!)
Click-track, I lean back, set the tone dirty and rough;
Play the solo of my life but
    the engineer's nodded off.
(He's got four chords and a capo in his case!)

The tour's arranged by hurling darts
    blindfold at a map
So it's "Goodnight, Wembley!",
    "Hello, Cumberland Gap!"
(He's got four chords and a capo in his case!)
There's a dream in my mind, it chills as well as thrills
There's a beat in my heart, and gold in them thar tills
(He's got four chords and a capo in his case!)

Yeah! Punch the air, kick some ass and hit the road.
Shove off, shufflers;
    obey the My Way Or The Highway Code.
Off my face!
(He's got four chords and a capo in his case!)

GNOMES OF BROMLEY

Come in if you're coming, welcome to Duncarin;
There's a committee meeting that I'm chairing
Concerning the council overspending.
The residents are up in arms and feel penned in
By pillars of bureaucracy wrapped in red tape.
We say it's high time to give decent folk a break.
The bleeding hearts have bled us dry.
Pack them off to Cuba and give someone else a try.

And it's with the greatest humility
I can't see for the life of me why it can't be me.
I was on many a board of directors
Till Labour got in and thoroughly wrecked us.
It's time to elbow the spongers and
    boot out the failures –
Hang on, has someone been at my azaleas?
If you want peace then you've got to fight
And the ladder to success always leans to the right.

If all the bloody Reds
Come out from under the beds
They won't stop me,
No, they can't stop me;
They won't take my privet hedge
'Cos the first line of defence
Is The Gnomes Of Bromley,
The Gnomes Of Bromley!

The Gnomes Of Bromley are in the
    gardens of England
Guarding the greenhouse and pond.
They got where they are by sheer hard work
Not from some fairy waving a wand.

Come in, wipe your feet, that's what the mat's for.
Honestly, what do we pay our tax for?
I've seen how easily these Europeans swarm in
But in this neck of the woods there'll be no
    housewarming.
Civility and good manners will take an early bath
If any blighter dares to venture up my gravel path.
Eating our swans, selling bootleg porn?
Sorry, old fruit, it's hosepipes at dawn.

If these freeloading Communists
Have got me on their list
They won't stop me,
No, they won't top me;
They haven't reckoned
On my secret weapon –
It's The Gnomes Of Bromley
The Gnomes Of Bromley!

GOING SLOWHERE

Sofa over an airplane,
Jaguar in the hall,
Chicken in the oven,
Ducks on the wall.
A feather duster, tickle under there
Round and round the garden, going slowhere.

Whistles in the wardrobe,
Trainers on the mat,
Football on the radio.
In your mitt, a cup of gnat's.
If you want some, the pot's over there
Going cold, going slowhere.

Brontosaurus in the bathroom,
Zombie on the bed,
Jesus on the fridge door
With a monkey on his head.
Who came first? God, who really cares?
Unbelievable, going slowhere.

The Tilburys are hung up
St. Michael's on the line.
A bottle of clarity's disappeared
And everything looks fine.
Retired and emotional, here come the stairs
Head for Bedfordshire, going slowhere.

HALF-LIFE

We make the effort to hook up
Occasionally
And we'd wonder the cafes
And galleries.
Make light of the shadows that we see
Splash in the puddles
And go Dutch on the teas.

And we'd stroll
Through Soho
Though we know
There's nowhere to go
For us - together
For us - no, never
For us - no, never again.

Of course, I'd never admit it
But, yes, I suppose I still love you
(There, you see, I just did it)
But in a different way than I used to.

The crowds of couples kissing
In the bazaars
In theatres, restaurants,
Bus stops and bars.
Perhaps they'll be lucky and float up to the stars.
I hope they're lucky and not end up where we are.

And we stare
In shop panes clear.
You're right there,
I'm wrong here.
Look at us – together
Look at us – no, never
Look at us – no, never again.

I'm too shy to convey it
But, yes, I suppose I love you
(I'd have to be drunk to say it)
But not as completely as I used to.

HAPPY BIRTHDAY TO YOU

Standing on the courtroom step
Will someone please give me a cigarette?
I gave them up for the kids and her
Now I need to see something else get burned
And go up in smoke, then left flat by a soulless boot
...Happy birthday to you.

Standing in my least worst clothes
Seeing her take the house tied up in bows.
Happy never after for this black-hearted baddie
Here comes Prince Charming, my girls' new daddy
Handsome and dashing, driving to their rescue
...Happy birthday to you.

Happy birthday to you
Every day's a happy birthday to you
Enjoy the present, return the past
Happy birthday...I hope it's your last.

In his car on the forecourt
I can see you shuddering
But you got what you wanted
I've lost all I had
Surely it's me who should be blubbering
And suffering?
Come on, admit it
That you loved me once
When we were daft and we laughed
Before we turned into cunts.

The realisation's smacked me in the head;
The girl I would have died for – has left me for dead.

I've got to pay you to clothe and feed
Children you won't let me see.
It sticks in my throat to mention
You're taking half my pension.
I gave you my youth –
    now you've taken my future too
...Happy birthday to you.

Happy birthday to you
Every day's a happy birthday to you
Enjoy the present, return the past
Happy birthday...I hope it's your last.

HELLO, CAN I HELP YOU?

Hello, can I help you?
What do you want me to say
About my friend who died today?
Conversation becomes a monologue...

Hello?

You're not going to see me
Wailing poor poetry
With a tear-stained guitar strumming
And if you want me to do
A breakdown in public view
You've got another think coming.

Hello, can I help you?

You know how it is
And if you don't, you will
Tiptoe through this emotional minefield
Grief is that hole love falls down
When it has nowhere to go
Hello?

It's not a good time
Is it ever a good time?
But there will be good times again

Hello

HUMPHREY GO-KART (I FORGOT)

Don't ask me my date of birth
It's such a long time ago
Don't ask me my real name
Quite honestly, I just don't know.
Was it Cairo Fred, Vienna Tom
Or Twelve-Sombreros Joe?
But I do know that Laurel & Hardy's first names
Were definitely Curly and Moe.

Don't dig around for diaries
I don't recall any being kept.
Nope, I don't remember the first time I laughed
Or the last time I wept.
Was I in the Top Ten charts for five years straight?
Was I slipped a million dollar bung?
And who was the dude I was handcuffed to for
    30 years?
Ah, it's on the tip of my tongue.

How did I get all that I've got?
Did I sire 90 kids and name them all Randolph Scott?
Did I scoop the 10 million quid lottery jackpot?
I forgot.

Don't poke around for poetry
I don't know how to rhyme.
I can't recite a Shakespeare soliloquy
Or sing 'Buddy, Can You Spare A Cent?'
Have I met any of my wives?

Do I know if water's wet?
Does Quasimodo ring a bell?
Oh, I know this one! No, I forget...

Who won the World Cup in 1966?
What's that old thing that can't be taught new tricks?
Did I compile the *International Who's Who Of*
What's What?
I forgot.

Did I find the meaning of life and then lose the plot?
Was I struck by lightning in a Vegas parking lot?
Gimme a clue - am I ice cold or getting hot?
I forgot.

Did Philip Barlow play Humphrey Go-Kart?
How much is an item found in a Poundshop?
What's the name of the land where there's a
multitude of Scots?
I forgot.

I WANT ONE, TOO

Daniella's got one
Mariella's got one
Mr Weller's got one
And I want one, too

Gemma's got a square one
The price a far-from-fair one
Emma's got a rare one
And I want one, too

I got to have it, have it, have it, have it
have it, have it, have it, *have it now!!!!*
So give me, give me, give me, give me
give me, give me, give me, give me.
Have it, have it, have it, have it
have it, have it, have it, *have it now!!!!*
Right with me, with me, with me, with me
with me, with me, with me, with me.

Daniella's got a neat one
Mariella's got a sweet one
Mr Weller's got a petite one
And I want one, too

Jackie's got a red one
Taki's got the best one
I have got a question:
Can I have one, too?

I got to have it, have it, have it, have it
have it, have it, have it, *have it now!!!!*
So give me, give me, give me, give me
give me, give me, give me, give me.
Have it, have it, have it, have it
have it, have it, have it, *have it now!!!!*
Right with me, with me, with me, with me
with me, with me, with me, with me.

And now at last I've got one
Yes, it's true, I've got one
And now I've finally got one:
What does it do?

I WAS HAPPY HERE

Work is work and play is work
And a child is work and love is work
Relaxing's work and shopping's work
And food is work and thinking's work
Walking's work and talking's work
And understanding's work and sleep is work
Communicating's work and hate is work
And sex is work and nothing's work.

Ambition's work and failing's work
And moving's work and staying's work
Strength is work and fear is work
And the past is work and the future's work
Smoking's work and drinking's work,
Unemployment's work, enjoyment's work
Crime is work and driving's work
And war is work and freedom's work.

I was happy here
I was someone
I was no-one
I was happy here.
I was happy here.
I knew where I was going
I knew where I was staying
I was happy here
I was happy here.

You were my friend
I was your friend.
I was happy here
I was happy here.

I was happy here.

I WORK IN A SHOP

Lickspittle fuckwit'll do as he's hit,
Jobsequious battery chickenshit.
Earplugs and beermugs, cool in the shades,
A tick on the list, this is afraid.

Home is a stone arse with multiple holes.
Work is jerking hands on dead genitals.
Talk is sad laughs and loops of complaint.
Staining the brain like smoke on old paint.

Monday is bollocks, Tuesday's the shits,
Wednesday's a pisser, Thursday is tits,
Friday is arseholes, Saturday's a fart,
Sunday is cunt day, then it's back to the start.

She's ambulatory, I'm so-socialist.
On the other hand, there is a fist.
The perpetual grin of a laboratory ape.
Love is a socially accepted form of rape.

Clock in, watch out,
    inside there's an unfulfillable chasm.
All the porn in the world can't bring you to orgasm.
Work on the way to work with a working lunchtime.
If life's a joke, give me the punchline.

Monday is bollocks, Tuesday's the shits,
Wednesday's a pisser, Thursday is tits,
Friday is arseholes, Saturday's a fart,
Sunday is cunt day, then it's back to the start.

I.C.U.

I got you, your email
And your password, too
And your secret viewing habits,
Don't deny it isn't true.
With the malware we installed
We've seen you watch those titties bounce
It was easy to get our hands
On your online accounts.

I... C... U...

What we made was a double-screen
Time-dated video
Where we can see you stare at the glare
Of a captive, punished ho'
We'll spare you the squalid details
We're all aware what you've seen
Although we've found out in our research
She wasn't quite sixteen

Wouldn't you love to love to have
Someone to confide in?
Wouldn't you love to love to have
Some hole you can hide in?
I... C... U...
I... C... U...

Thought your reputation pure as snow
Now you're white as a sheet
And your future will be blind-eye black
If we're not in receipt
Of five grand in Bitcoin
We order you to give
In six days to this address
(Case sensitive).

Wouldn't you love to love to have
Someone to confide in?
Wouldn't you love to love to have
Some hole you can hide in?
Wouldn't you love to love to have
Someone to confide in?
Wouldn't you love to love to have
Some hole you can hide in?
I... C... U...
I... C... U...

I'M A LOSER

I can tell so much by your sighs
I can tell so much in your kiss goodbyes:
I'm a loser.
Found out I don't matter to you that much
It don't affect you that we lost touch:
I'm a loser.

I know the future's mine for the taking
But I can't be bothered.
I know the future's mine for the making
But I can't be arsed.
I'm a loser!

I've been through a whole lot of changes
I've seen how friends become strangers:
Dismissed as a loser.
The birds are singing in the trees
They sing their song but not for me:
I'm a loser

I know the future's mine for the taking
But I can't be bothered.
I know the future's mine for the making
But I can't be arsed.
I'm a loser!

IN SOMEONE'S HANDS

Why do you see me as inhuman?
I only do what everyone's doing
To buy some basic food to chew and
Send some money back home

To my family, I so miss them
I don't know when I'll see them again –

But for now I have to work 15 hours a day
In the wind and the rain
And I can't complain
For only five hours' pay.

Don't accuse me of putting you out on the dole.
I can't argue about things that are beyond our
control.
What will it take to make you understand
We're manipulated like putty in someone's hands?
We're all numbers on a sheet,
Pieces of meat,
Putty in someone's hands.

I like your cuppa, your runny egg sandwich
I'm learning to speak your language
And trying to forget the damage
That forced me to leave home.

My loving family, I so miss them
Every day is like Mother's Day and I'm an orphan—

But I got to work 15 hours a day
In the wind and the rain
And I can't complain
For only five hours' pay.

Don't accuse us of stealing all your jobs.
Blame them in the penthouses,
    private planes and yachts.
What will it take to make you understand
We're manipulated like putty in someone's hands?
We're all numbers on a sheet,
Pieces of meat,
Putty in someone's hands.

INVASION OF B.S.

It's just like any Saturday morning
Brilliantly dull, fascinatingly boring
Bells buzzed, doors knocked by the uniforms
Him and him and her and her forming swarms
Big trucks, tiny cars with somewhere to go
Last night's litter show the wind which way to blow

No sudden revolution, no instant coup d'etat
Overall mood is mellow, it's tres petit-bourgeois
From abattoirs to coffee bars,
      it's flowing, running smooth
Put the needle on the record, we're all in the groove
There's a subtle difference
      I can't quite put my finger on
Inner voice says it's something best not to linger on

We take our usual table at the Lick-Quid barterie
Greasy window, big cardiacs attacking main artery
No cheese of Apollo, no pub quislings,
      Metro gnomes; we banter
We exuberate, the ant of brilli waves
      the stick of Fanta
Earwigging patrons sneer at us or fume or fret
It fearises them to know they haven't got us yet

We're not the only ones who know what love is
We're not the only ones who know

INVITATION TO A BEHEADING

Double-crossed and dotted
By wink of eye as flies were swatted
By mine host's catamite and butler
(Previous employer: Randolph Hutler)
Universally voted the El Guapo
Of the shaven Aryan gay Gestapo
Gliding silently through the proceedings
Heeding scarlet gashes bleeding
White teeth and lies and laughter
And after...?

As the prime cuts are devoured
We gather which English roses were deflowered.
Were they and cameras loaded?
Whose flashgun prematurely exploded?
Chinese whispers round the houses
Raising glasses, dropping trousers.
Run her ragged round the flagpole,
Tied and gagged on a maypole.
A souvenir of the ones we had;
So glad...

High on balloons of brandy,
Stick a joint in the bust of Gandhi.
Elegant fixtures designed by "Oh, who is it?"
Ebony toothpicks? How exquisite!
The bore's talk of austerity
Is cause for prolonged hilarity.

Cruel appetites had been whetted
But the main event could not be bettered.
Then Danton suggests re-enactment games –
Home, James...

IT'S TIME I WENT MAD AGAIN

Wheels go round except when they don't.
A wicket keeper keeps a wicket.
The meaning of life can never be found,
Just like your winning lottery ticket.
Leaves fall in autumn and grow again in spring.
A kingdom generally has at least one king.
But without love, life's a yawn;
It's as uniform as a manicured lawn.
I'm fed up chewing olden flakes of scorn,
It's time I went mad again.

Rain is wet and falls out of a thing
In the sky called a cloud.
Noise can be heard by creatures who have
    working ears
And you'll always spot people in a crowd.
Siamese twin eunuchs couldn't give two fucks
And stuff that sucks sucks.
But without love, life's so orderly;
I'm as bored with it as it's bored of me.
Tranquillised by tranquility,
It's time I went mad again.

I want to count the letters,
Let the bad times forget us,
I want the straight lines broken and curving;
I want to think with my heart,
Put a full stop at the start
Of the life sentence I wish to be serving.

Drunk drivers drive when they're drunk.
Painters paint paintings with paint.
Sunny days are hot and cold ones are not.
What is is and what ain't ain't.
Statues are made of heroes and dictators.
Chips and crisps are made of potatoes.
But without love, life's predictable
Like a goal scorer who has kicked a ball.
Where is the wonderful?
It's time I went mad again.

IVY

Invite to attend the pitiful ritual
I don't wanna
I don't wanna
Rubber-necking whiners, cheese and vitriol
I'm not gonna
I'm not gonna

"But what if everyone felt that way?"
"Then I'd be a fool to feel any other way"
I don't wanna
I don't wanna

Backs slapped, hands clapped, eyes on the prize
In whose honour?
In whose honour?
Jobs slashed, mobs flashed, smiling through the lies
I don't wanna
I don't wanna

When doing the unexpected is expected of you
There's no way out way out enough that you can do
And I don't wanna
I don't wanna

JOIN THE QUEUE

Another bad attack of good memories;
Wouldn't life be cool if you could make time freeze?
You were The One To Watch and
great things'll happen
But all those dreams turned to crap an'
You're in a limbo where the plain fact is
We forgot you were the tape-breasting Billy Whizz.
And here you are now, the non-runner Never Was
Why didn't you reach your potential, kid?
"Well, because—"

Rigsby impressions no longer impress,
Your punchlines require an archaeologist's guess,
No-one here's heard of Will Hay, Hylda Baker or
Rudolf Hess.

There's nothing - nothing you can say
There's nothing - nothing you can do
Join the queue.

You were the nutter at school, the total crease.
Bullies would be breathless, begging you to cease.
Making love to a fresh-planted sapling
Had the Drama beak squeak, "It's worthy of Chaplin."
Blank pages, bare stages, day dream ambitions,
Days became decades of wasted wishing.
Non-achievement, no bereavement,
slate wiped clean;
You didn't have it in you to be a has-been.

Could've been a pop star
    'cept you're fat and can't sing.
Bad breath, tone deaf, can't pluck a string,
And that one song you wrote was
    painfully self-pitying.

There's nothing – nothing you can say
There's nothing – nothing you can do
Join the queue.

At the school reunion do for The Class Of Whenever
All the creeps you mocked turned out awfully clever;
Kaye's Senior Editor of Channel 4 News,
Sue's a style guru, Tim's big in orthopaedic shoes.
Murray made a mint;
    that fat cat knew when to pounce.
Jez takes a call concerning offshore accounts.
One by one they turn on you with smiles sadistic:
"How droll! You're on the dole? Is one a statistic?"

It's not that everyone was better than you,
It's just they were hungrier and
    they knew what to chew.
Whilst you were climbing walls they were climbing
    ladders, paying dues.

There's nothing – nothing you can say
There's nothing – nothing you can do
Join the queue.

KEEPING MUM

She calls the plasma a telly and the radio a tranny,
Recalls when Cliff wasn't the
    Christmas Number One.
She spent the first half of her life
    plucking her eyebrows
And the second painting them back on.
And Samuel the goldfish patrols his bowl,
Wide-eyed (of course) but still looking glum:
    He's keeping Mum.

Once, it was *Woman's Realm* and then
    Woman's Weekly,
Now it's *OK!* and *Chat* and the freebie TV guide.
No letters on the mat,
    it's either pizza or curry leaflets
Or a pamphlet saying for whom Christ died.
And Emma comes round to deal with the bills,
It's gotten hard to do the sums:
    She's keeping Mum.

Above the rooftops of London
The high rises, chimney stacks,
A permanently changing sky moves in hues
Of red, white, blue and black.
And those below who go to and fro
And wouldn't think to look at it twice
To try to find some peace of mind
And define a paradise...

She enters the room,
      forgets what she went there for.
Whatever it was, someone else has them.
Softly grinding her hips into the mattress
To the sound of next door's lovers' orgasm.
And I drop by – "Under protest," she says,
A game of Scrabble, coffees laced with rum:
      I'm keeping Mum.

KEEPS

They say there's a stairway to Heaven,
I think I'll take the lift.
Money can't buy love so masturbation
Was my concession to thrift.
I don't want to go to Chelsea's Flower Show
Hob-nobbing 'mongst the lobelias,
Or ogling the pain-in-the-Ascot titfers:
"Look at the size of Cecilia's!"

I'm at the door to the sweetheart of the city,
I ring the bell, it turns to dust.
The breadhead next door is toasting himself,
He's on the dole and off his crust.
I hope I'm a cut above her past parade of creeps.
Maybe for this three-time loser, this one's for keeps.

Don't twitter the buzz about the birds and bees,
Tell me about the birds and blokes.
All I've ever heard is ha-ha hoo-hoo hee-hee;
All of my best friends are jokes.
The last cracker I managed to pull
Was at a one-man Christmas do;
The paper crown didn't fit, my new trousers split
And my family sent an I.O.U.

I hear the beat of the sweetheart of the city
And her rhythm's in time with mine.
I spent too long composing the world's saddest song
Trying to get the words to scan.

Mouth dry as an AA alkie but
    from an eye saltwater seeps;
Maybe this time, for this three-time loser,
    this one's for keeps.

'Cos of my vanity I don't know what she sees in me –
Teeth coming loose, hair falling out.
In my optical daze I was a slimline tonic,
Then I became bitter and stout.
Like a lighter, she's ignited in me
Something like that something called love,
Something I'd hard convinced myself that
I was incapable of.

Let's go and get those tattoos now,
The ones we may not live to regret
While the flowers of the morning
And the backs of our ears are still wet.
Let's lose our doubts and inhibitions,
    let lying dogs sleep.
Ah-ha... This one's for keeps.

KOLIBRI

The envelope was tramp tooth brown,
Stabbed on its back, a blood red wax seal.
Slitting the side, I removed ghost white paper,
Unfolded it to reveal
The names of well-heeled debauched perverts,
Plotters and traitors to the State.
I reached for the death black telephone
And consigned them to their fate.

I dialled the number,
The receiver purred.
A friendly voice said, "What's the word?"
... "Hummingbird."

I hoisted myself out of my chair,
Limped across my office to the fireplace.
In the mirror the glow of the flames
Dance in the bones and hollows of my face.
I brushed the dandruff from my shoulders,
Pick a strand of blond hair from my trousers
And I ejaculated on my father
To visions of dead men in burning houses.

I dialled the number,
The receiver purred.
A friendly voice said, "What's the word?"
... "Hummingbird."

Eleven years on I kill myself,
Cremated with cans of paraffin.
But beware, you dogs, the game's not over;
I am airborne and what you're breathing.
I'm in the syringe of pancuronium bromide,
Pentobarbital and potassium chloride.
I'm the power in the chair that gets you fried.
I'm the hot air that moves waves of genocide.

I dialled the number,
The receiver purred.
A friendly voice said, "What's the word?"
... "Hummingbird."

LET ME PAINT A PICTURE FOR YOU

As I tend each paintbrush bristle
I give a little whistle
With lips that long to kiss all
My memories hello.
Not even if you pay or dare me
Would I climb Blood Hill - *scary* -
But here I am and solitary;
Watch out down below!

Let me paint a picture for you,
See the world from my point of view.
Not an abstract or a caricature;
An untainted vision, clear and pure.
Care to inspect the sketches in my bureau?
Figures caught in chiaroscuro?
Let me paint a picture for you.

Stay here, a warm gentle breeze all
Day, no need for an easel;
Lay my pad on my knees'll
Do comfortably for me.
Surrounded by my paintbox clutter,
A round of tea and bread and butter.
The sound of crow wings flutter
Above but he won't claw me.

Let me paint a picture of you,
Every line a road or a clue.

It's my personal perspective
(If you don't like it I'll correct it).
It's probably better up the other way.
What are you prepared to pay
For me to paint a picture of you?

Climbing up up up,
Never stop stop stop
To the top top top
Of Blood Hill.
What a scene scene scene,
The rolling green green green
Strong as poteen 'teen 'teen
Drawn from a still.

I spied the crofter's daughter
Down on paper and I caught her
But a small-town big-shot picked her up for a song
...Though the hands were all wrong.

Let me paint a picture for you;
Dazzle brushwork, varied in hue.
I'm not immune to critics' derision –
They can get lost in my composition.
Dry theorists fly when I splash wet-in-wet.
Can you see what it is yet?
Let me paint a picture –
– pour a tincture –
After I paint a picture for you.

LOOK AFTER

Well, he used to have a job
and he used to love his job
then he had to quit his job
to look after his dad, Bob
and he looked after his dad, Bob
until his dad, Bob, died.

Do's and functions, there were some
but more than some, he did not come
the reason gave to every one
he had to look after his mum
and he looked after his mum
until his mum died.

And then he would get up early
to look after his girly, Shirley...

And no matter how hard the wind changed
        and turned cold
and blew straight in his eye
he did not cry.

MARWAR JUNCTION

We met on the level
Passed on the square
We're together but not together
We're here but not all there
And there's an invite
Tonight
To a fungus function
But both of us
Will miss the bus
We've got to meet a man at Marwar Junction

Blind drunk behind the shades
Cancel the morning after
'Cos if we stop we'll disappear
And you can't frame laughter.
Freedom's an open-air dungeon
Marwar Junction.

What at first
Sounded prosaic
Became the worst
Obvious and formulaic.
Are we cursed
To wander this mosaic
For infinity?

We’re not together now we’re together
We’re all there but not there
We’re spiralling in different circles
And both of them are square.
And the kids are dreaming
Screaming
Hair-pulling and air-punching
And I’m beside myself
At Marwar Junction
I’m beside myself
At Marwar Junction
I’m beside myself...

MENINGITIS (DANCE FOR ME)

Here we are, darling,
In our dream cottage in Commodious Parva
Cardiganned, slippered,
Promoted to the ranks of grandmother and -father.
It's lukewarm still waters now
After life on a white-knuckle whitewater rafter
It's feet up, eyes down
For a dull house in shabbily happy ever after.

What's life got left in store for us?
Oh, there's plenty more for us
It's written out plain in large print
So we don't have to squint

There'll be arthritis, laryngitis –
On that we silently agree;
Tendonitis, tell St. Vitus to save...
    the last dance for me
        (If you don't outlive me...)

Here we are, darling
I think I've figured out – the remote control
This is on, this is off
This is loud, this is soft – the rest I still don't know.
It's high time we tried our prune wine
Tonight we can really let rip
And what a surprise
The chemist has supplies of
    Anusol and denture-grip.

Yesteryear, drunk on freedom's beer
We railed against boredom's reign
Now we sleep around the clock
And we'd fan-dabby-dozily do it again.

There'll be meningitis, tonsilitis -
On that we silently agree;
Conjunctivitis...
Tell St. Vitus to save...
      the last dance for me
            (If you don't outlive me.
            Sadness definitively
            If you're not with me)

We injected them marijuanas
We puffed on them cocaines
We snorted up them acids
Until they boiled our brains.

What's life got left in store for us?
Oh, there's plenty more for us
Forget politricks and who sold us out
We've got all this to shout about:

There'll be arthritis, laryngitis -
On that we silently agree
Tendonitis, tell St. Vitus to save...
The last dance for me.

Here we are, darling,
Our dream cottage in Commodious Parva…

MONEY IN THE HAT

(A dialogue between a boulevardier and a busker)

I've a wife, an ex-wife,
A mistress and a brat
    Shut your trap
    Put the money in the hat
I'm down to the Tuscany villa
The country pile and Chelsea flat
    Shut your trap
    Put the money in the hat

Pranged the yacht in the harbour
While docking at Cap Ferrat
    Shut your trap
    Put the money in the hat
From Glastonbury to Glyndebourne
One's always where it's at
    Shut your trap
    Put the money in the hat

    Put the money in the hat
    Put the money in the hat
    Do you think I like doing this
    You cosy, dozy prat?
    I'm down on my uppers
    Can't buy a cuppa, that's a fact
    So whip out your wallet
    And put the money in the hat

I played squash with David Gilmour
And he kindly signed my Strat
    Shut your trap
    Put the money in the hat
In the Royal Enclosure at Ascot
The corgi got a pat
    Shut your trap
    Put the money in the hat

Sorry, I don't carry cash
Accept PayPal? Oh drat!
    Shut your trap
    Put the money in the hat
Could I have a receipt
So I can claim it back on VAT?
    Shut your trap
    Put the money in the hat

    Put the money in the hat
    Put the money in the hat
    Are you deaf as a post
    Or blind as a bat?
    There's a little green-eyed idol
    But no-one cares for that
    For the good of my health, share your wealth
    And put the money in the hat

MOON RISING OVER LONDON

When I wake up tomorrow
    I'll be in someone else's bed,
And my head will be splitting
    from the things I never said.
You'll be thinking of the future and I'll be history –
When the moon rises over London
    and the sun sets on me.

I can see them swarm around me
    like they've got something to find,
And I know if I was like them
    you'd be the last thing on my mind.
I've got one last question:
    "What did you want me to be
Before the moon rose over London
    and the sun set on me?"

I can't pin down the memory,
    keep it framed up on the shelf.
May what you wish on others be all you get yourself.
I can't tell if I'm lonely without you
    or if I'm finally free –
When the moon rises over London
    and the sun sets on me.

MONSTERS MUST BE DESTROYED

Working double-shift at the In and Out
Meatpackers in a line till the milking hour shout.
Happiness undefined
In the daily grind.

I came out here following the shadow of DeNiro.
A year after losing my shirt my income's
    dropped a zero.
I should've resigned
When I was behind.

I've cock-slapped the girls
Now I'm turning on the boys.
Hollywood made us monsters
And monsters must be destroyed.

Living on strawberries, amyl nitrate and 'zac.
Staying hard ain't easy on a Teflon-coated rack.
Scraping the rind
In 4/4 time.

How can I tell my folks I'm respectable
When all they see is my shaven testicles?
Pick up the slack;
Get humping, Jack.

I've cock-slapped the girls
Now I'm turning on the boys.
Hollywood made us monsters
And monsters must be destroyed.

Banging, banging, banging
      to get white blood out my rocks
Then the continuity girl says
      I'm wearing different socks.
We'll have to take it again;
Don't shrink, my violet friend.

At home in the evening with the missus, smoking kif
"Let's get it on so get 'em off,"
      she says but I'm bored stiff.
Ain't my head that aches;
Too much porn flakes.

Love all, new balls please,
Score - bored - null and void.
Hollywood made us monsters
And monsters must be destroyed.

MR POTTER OF CREEP ST.

Every Friday, 11.17, you can set your alarm
When Mr Potter is thrown out of The Queen's Arms
After ten pints and juggling the landlady's
    chihuahuas;
Loses his balance on the kerb,
    squashing his bananas.
Lives round the corner on the first floor of
    5 Creep Street.
Only one visitor has been across the threshold –
    Plumber Pete
To repair a boiler in '94 – in the merry month of May;
He says he saw Mrs Potter that crisp and chilly day.
He couldn't give an accurate description
    but no-one's seen her since
Although on the landing
    there's the scent of lavender and mince.

Mr Potter! Mr Potter!

The word is Mr Potter's home is one ruled by
    iron-glove tyranny
And the neighbours whisper he made his pot with
    thin-grin villainy.
Even the mites and earwigs slink about on tip-toe.
Do the bathroom and kitchen taps dare to drip? No.
Even when he's out,
    Mrs Potter doesn't make a sound;

The reason why is, despite her size,
    her feet don't touch the ground.
No passer-by in Creep St. has ever seen her face
Poking through the curtain of tobacco-stained lace.
Downstairs say when music's heard,
    fit for a rigadoon
Only one pair of feet is heard
    on the ceiling of their front room.

Mr Potter! Mr Potter!

Mr Potter Saturday snoozes during the
    Gold Cup fixtures
As Mrs P walks through the wall to straighten
    all the pictures.
And though the dinner table is only set for one,
Mrs Potter is beside him to pass the time
    and parmesan.
Quinquagenarian, yes, but Mr and Mrs Potter
    still share the same bed
But there's no indentation on her pillow of her head.
They're the half-living proof that true love
    is immortal.
Mr Potter never speaks of it but we think he
    really ought to.
He can see right through her
    and she can read his mind.

They've got the best of both worlds;
    the real and undefined.
Despite Mrs P passing on it was merely physically.
Mr Potter never gave up the ghost;
    he still loves her spiritually.

Mr Potter! Mr Potter!

MY DRUGLY PAST (PART 2)

Pale wondering twilight.
Not my scene; too shy, might
Slink into the gloom.
Wasps 'neath my skin,
Anti-hero heroin
Must slip out this sliding room.
But my head is like lead,
My legs pronounced dead,
Tongue won't wax prosaic,
My hands are on fire,
My clothes are barb wire,
My mind's a vandalised mosaic.
Astronaut monkey grinning,
Thought strand webs spinning
A puny verse.
In love, nothing's everything,
In hate, everything's nothing,
And life's a curse.
Shimmering serenade,
Mundanity fade;
It's all too absurd.
Obsession to detail,
Confession is futile,
Fail to form the words.
The myriad of pills,
The thrills from curly bills,
Turn seconds into hours into moments into years.

The blow-back, the hot knife,
The high times with low life,
The crash from the sudden shift of gear.
Intestinal quaking,
Dust mouth, fingers shaking,
Distractions; I can't straight think.
Wave of paranoid terrors
Crash on my coast of errors,
Wash me away and down I sink
To my drugly past
In the human race I straggle in last...
To my drugly past
In the human race I crawl in last.

The uppers and downers,
The smilers, the frowners,
Cornered poet's pained refrain.
Conspiracy theorist
Connects the tenuous and merest
Links in an endless chain.
Please introduce me
To someone who'll seduce me
And doesn't even ask my name.
I don't know what mine is,
I'm a bag of smoke and jizz
With everyone but myself to blame.

When I descend from the acid
I'll be silent and placid –
A kicked jigsaw, no solution.
I can drown in the shallows,
The word of God rings hollow;
It's the gram delusion
Of my drugly past
In the human race I crawl in last...
To my drugly past
In the human race I straggle in last.

NEW UMBRELLA

You've got a new umbrella
How much did it cost?
What happened to the last one
- Stolen, broken or lost?
This one's very different
Looks like you've changed.
New umbrella
Old rain.

Stroll with your umbrella
The seafront promenade
The lane, the high street
Avenue, boulevard.
Seek shade from the sunshine
And its cancer and pain.
New umbrella
Old rain.

Let's see your new umbrella
Yes, it's stylish and nice.
Did you seek it out yourself
Or get professional advice?
Is your memory cleansed of the old one
Or does a stain remain?
New umbrella
Old rain.

NEXT

Hello, Eve, you can't see me
But I've focussed you in my mind.
I was your first and you were my first
And so we left the solo strumming days behind.

Us on a duvet, in the nude,
    on hot summer afternoons
Was time and energy well spent.
Then you picked up your knickers
    when the seat of learning called
And down the hall of empties you went.

You said, you said,
"This isn't the end, we'll stay good friends;
A weekend visit, an occasional text..."
NEXT!

Along came Jones, I jumped on your bones;
I was there to fill the interim.
When your fat husband worked away,
    we love rats would play
And you would never talk of him.

Dropping social graces,
    we got off our clothes and faces,
A *frottage a deux* on the QT,
But when you suggested something out of the blue
You suddenly lost all of your beauty:

You said, you said,
"He's bald and chubby, but my hubby
Fancies a threesome and he's highly sexed..."
NEXT!

Then there was Linds in the horn-rimmed bins.
We were pub rubbish, always trashed.
A few bottles of vino, getting obsceno,
The Fort Cortino's dash was well splashed.

Like Stan & Ollie or Kev & Lolly
We made an oddly perfect couple
Till you faced the saggy facts
    and cleaned up your act,
Joined the gym to get fit and supple.

You said, you said,
"I've taken up weights, kicked carbohydrates
Want to see my pecs when they're flexed?"
NEXT!

There was Beryl and Meryl and Sally and Sam.
There was Sharon and Karen and Pixie and Pam.
There was Doris (wife of Horace), there was Suki,
    and Reiko
There was Stacey and Tracy and Eric – *"Eric?"*
    – Big mistake!

And now there's just me and these memories
Of who I've had and what I've lost.
There's not a lot to live for or on
      now the money's gone
Up the wall, down the drain, casually tossed.

In the old folks home where the old groaners moan
Until their kids take them off in a hearse
I daily wash and shave on the off-chance of a rave
With a comely buxom nurse.

I say, I say,
"Wouldn't you rather have a spot of
      how's your father?"
And she looks at me perplexed...
"NEXT!"

NO FATHER, NO SON

The bright young things dissolve into shadows.
The women turn blue, framed in broken windows.
My head lolls forward and my eyes roll back.
A case of dead faces place the cuts and the tracks.
Suffocating in the dead air kisses,
Defecating a ream of paper promises.
Baby, nipple nibble, eyes pinned to a brooch,
Green as Surrey, fat as a coach,
When words were noises, stupid as the sun,
Fingers were meat trees, naked for autumn.
Mumble mind jumble,
The end is hard as a gun.
I'll pass on with nothing to pass on.
No father, no son.

Toe the line, cut the acid, trip wires stop me.
When the vow breaks my baby will drop me
As time rips forward and the years drip back.
Damp rising, rotting all I wished for but lack.
From cot bars to sot bars, opportunity knocked,
Keys out of reach, the door stayed locked.
Old man, soup, droopy-eyed fixed on a blur;
Indeterminate, wish it was her.
Chances ran out like the cat who got run over.
Is this the last straw or a no-leaf clover?
Undertakers overtake us,
The end is hard as a gun.
I'll pass on with nothing to pass on
No father, no son.

NOT YOUR PROPERTY

When I was a little boy
Who was it who broke my toys?
Who turned the sky from blue to black?
Who told the others to turn their backs
On me?
Who stuck in the knife and gave it a twist?
Thought with his cock and spoke with his fist?
Who spat on my dinner plate
And made a meal out of humiliating
Me?

I'm not your property
In your game of Monopoly.
Roll me out like dice on Park Lane
I'll take the money, you keep the pain.

It took a kiss to open my eyes
And see truth hunted by a pack of lies.
I remember sunlight dancing on the sea
When I was a boy, not your property.

Here I stand, only a man.
Scar tissues never tan.
Time warps and changes but what I fear
Is seeing you staring back in the mirror
At me.
'Cos no matter what life puts me through
I will never ever be like you.

I'll never stop loving my kids
I won't forget them like you did
With me.

I'm not your property
In your game of Monopoly.
Roll me out like dice on Park Lane
I'll take the losses, you keep the pain.

OLD BAG

        'IM: "See 'er?"
'IS MATE: "'Oo?"
        'IM: "'Er!"
'IS MATE: "'OO?"
        'IM: "There!"
'IS MATE: "Where?"
        'IM: *"THERE!!"*
'IS MATE: "Yeah...?"

'IM:
"Trudging along in dog-blanket clothes;
I tell you, she used to wear better than those.
But age and gravity have let her down, mate.
She used to be tasty, now she's past her sell-by date.

Quick, turn away, 'cos she's watching this way
If she clocked me after all this time,
    what could I say?
She was my first love, so dear to me, man;
Proud to hold her by my side, clutching my hand
But now she's an

OLD BAG – blowing down the street
OLD BAG – getting under your feet
OLD BAG – full of crap and wind
OLD BAG – stick it in the bin

... But give me a drink or ten
And her luck just might be in again..."

'ER: "See them?"
'ER MATE:"'Oo?"
'ER: "Them!"
'ER MATE:"Men?"
'ER: "Yeah."
'ER MATE:"Where?"
'ER: *"THERE!!"*
'ER MATE:"Yeah?"

'ER:
"See the one in the turn-ups on the left?
Stick a mullet on his red slaphead,
Take 12 inches off that gone-to-waist,
Take a chin or three from under that face.

Looks like only Stella's touched his lips
And skips of chips have gone straight to his hips.
He's the one who said, 'There's no-one else.'
Put me on a pedestal then left me on the shelf.
I fell for his

OLD BLAG - sweeping me off my feet
OLD BLAG - sweet-talking piece of meat.
Now he's an
OLD SAG - gy-faced soak with his cans in an
OLD BAG - gripped in his shaky hand

... But if he wants a sympathy shag
He can grab the love handles of this old bag..."

OLD DOG

I should have seen it coming
In the tealeaves and the cards,
Sung by the sirens,
Written by the bards.
My mind should have stopped my heart
Pounding that old blue beat.
Life was an undone jigsaw puzzle
I hoped this piece would complete.

Old door, new keys
(Never again will I jump to its chime)
Old dog, new fleas
(Never again – till the next time)

I've got deja-vu and insomnia
Simultaneously.
I call you Anna Stesia
For all the feeling you had for me.
Is there a handle on my back?
Or something written on my face?
They say "It's a small world"; is that why
I always end up in this place?

Soft sell, hard cheese
(There's no new fire without a bright spark)
Old dog, new fleas
(I'm scratching in the dark)

The Gossips want the lowdown
But I can't say it's your fault.
I made the bait and set the trap
But I ended up being caught.
No more derision, just division,
That's half of what I want to say.
Half a pair - half in love
And half a world away.

New cure, old disease
(These thirsty leeches will have me bleed)
Old dog, new fleas
(Will somebody take the lead?)
Old door, new keys
(Never again will I jump to its chime)
Old dog, new fleas
(Never again - till the next time)

ONE TOMORROW

As dawn crawls across the morning-after bed
There's the murmured suggestion of your head
On this pillow.
And the sheets hold hard the perfume you sprayed;
I will inhale it now 'cos it will fade
One tomorrow.

As light creeps across lovers' dispersed detritus
Revealing dark desires in its unforgiving brightness,
A shade of sorrow
As I contemplate a heart as empty as my hand.
I'll keep both open for your return
One tomorrow.

And outside there's the everyday kind
On their way, in their way
... Coping...
And inside every everyday mind
On their way, in their way
They're hoping, hoping...

As dusk descends and birds and traffic quieten
Bid adieu to the few who terrify and frighten
And leave us hollow.
Face to face, embracing you embracing me.
Is there a future? Close our eyes and we will see
One tomorrow.

PRETEND

Gone are the days when we were the kings.
We smashed our sandcastles and spoilt everything.

Whatever it was that bound us together,
There's little trace of it now.
As little boys we pledged friendship forever
But now it's buried by distance's doubt
And "Now you mean nothing to me."

Your mates convince you we were just a phase
That all kiddiewinkies go through.
They surround you like a swarm of buzzing flies
And beat me with backhanded abuse
And "You don't fit no more."

What did you want to be?
Can't you remember?
What did you want to achieve?
Oh, don't you know?

I know you'll close your eyes
And pretend you don't care,
But who'll mend your head
When you fall down the stairs?

What do you think at the end of the day?
Are you scared your friends will turn you away?
At the end of the day, what do you think
As you retrieve the ashtray from the kitchen sink?
You don't light up no more.

What did you want to be?
Don't give me that empty gaze.
What will you do with your life?
Don't throw it all away.

I know you'll close your eyes
And pretend you don't care
But when you look around again
Who will be there?

Gone are the days when we were the kings.
We smashed our sandcastles and spoilt everything.
Now we content ourselves by acting the goat,
Abdicating our titles and throwing up in the moat.

PUKE BLOOOZ

Got puke on mah fingahz!
(*YEAHHHHH!!!!!!*)
Got puke on mah nose!
(*YEAHHHHH!!!!!!*)
Got puke on mah elbow!
(*YEAHHHHH!!!!!!*)
Got puke on mah toes!
(*YEAHHHHH!!!!!!*)

Oh baby, I got da puke bloooz!
Oh baby baby, oh fucking Christ,
 I got dem puke bloooz, yeah yeah!

Got puke on mah forehead!
(*YEAHHHHH!!!!!!*)
Got puke on mah watermelon!
(*YEAHHHHH!!!!!!*)
Got puke on mah ice cream!
(*YEAHHHHH!!!!!!*)
Fuckin' hell, I got puke everywhere!

Oh baby baby, I got da puke bloooz!
Oh Jesus Christ oh baby,
 I got dem ol' puke bloooz, yeah yeah!

PUNK IS CRAP

Punk is crap, Metal's crap,
Reggae's crap, Rap is crap
Folk is crap, Jazz is crap,
Electro's crap, Prog is crap.

What have you got
That isn't utter rot?
Capitalism
Materialism
Islamism
It's all jism
Fascism
Zionism
LOVE IS THE THING
HATE ISN'T.

Christ is crap, *The Sun* is crap,
The Mail is crap, *The Guardian*'s crap
The Times is crap, The past is crap,
The present's crap, The future's crap.

What have you got
That isn't utter rot?
Cynicism
Sexism
Feminism
Just dismiss 'em
Atheism
Racism

LOVE IS THE THING
HATE ISN'T.

Dope is crap, Drink is crap,
Food is crap, Books is crap,
Film is crap, Fashion's crap,
Comedy's crap, Poetry's crap.

What banner can unite
Where no-one will fight?
Patriotism
Communism
Idealism
It's all egotism
Separatism
Nationalism
LOVE IS THE THING
HATE ISN'T.

RATER RATER

Four star mattress
Two star dream
Three star sunshine
Five star coffee bean
Four star bacon
Three star eggs
One star romance
Five star sex

RATER! RATER!
Don't wait till later
RATER! RATER!
Accumulator
We – Must – KNOW!

Five star razor
Two star soap
Four star blazer
Three star dope
Two star taxi
Four star shoes
Three star gravel
Five star mews

RATER! RATER!
Analyse the data
RATER! RATER!
Aggregator
We – Must – KNOW!

Three star review
Two star book
Five star reception
One star martini – shook!
Three star speeches
Five star free bar
Four star one-to-one with
Two-face star

RATER! RATER!
Was it cheesy? Was it greater?
RATER! RATER!
Mass culture tabulator
We – Must – KNOW!
We – Must – KNOW!

RE:UNION

The trees are charred skeletal hands clawing
    a dead grey sky
And I reluctantly put on my old school tie.
A parade of bores in party hats whose jokes
    and politics were blue;
The warm beer scene froze when I saw you.
The lines at school and the lines of speed
    are now etched around our eyes,
But our jawlines disappeared in the
    avalanche of pies.
The way you licked the crumbs from your lips
    and whistled some old tune
Brought back double French in the afternoons.
The yawn-again drullards bury hatchets, dig up folk,
And I joined you outside for a smoke.
Our plumes of fumes met and melded,
    frolic and fade in the air;
You broke the quiet and whispered,
    "Do you still care?"
We made light of our darkening days,
    how times turned numb, mundane,
But are families and work wholly to blame?
Outside three more gins, I said, "Let's go for a spin,
    your knee-high boots I long to fill.
If your husband don't get us, then only cancer will."

SALMON PINK RAINCOAT

It's your salmon pink raincoat,
Its belt tied in a loose knot.
It's for me to find what lies beneath
And take and taste all you've got.
That's correct, stand defiant,
As your worthless servant kneels.
Slip your belt from its loops and whip me
As I gratefully kiss your high heels.

Let me, let me lick your stockings,
Let my hands hold, roam and hunt.
Let my face into the folds of your raincoat
And inhale the perfume of your cunt.
May my eyes be permitted to look up
At your horizon eyes, your cruel smile?
Tear open your white silk blouse, I implore you
So I may suck your breasts like a child.

The curve in your waist as you reach for the bottle,
The warmth of the wine as it slips from your tongue
    to mine.
The intensity and heat of our embracing
Lit up by midnight moonshine.
Nude now apart from your jewellery,
The sweat of slaves clothe your fingers and throat;
From haughty to whore, come on, talk dirty.
Don't relent, torment me with insults.

Between your thighs, I'm lapping and drinking;
Let my hunger feed you what you need.
Slip your belt around my neck and choke me,
Dig your nails deep and drag, I need to bleed.
Grab your hair, turn the tables,
Force you down, now you bow to me.
Gripping your wrists, your face in contortions
As I take you sweetly and violently.

We're married, yes, but we still enjoy this –
Turning you from a wild cat to a tamed pet.
As I recline to enjoy you do my bidding
I light one of your Consulate cigarettes.
Through ghost-white smoke, I watch you
On your knees happily giving head.
The phone rings, I answer; it's my daughter
With three little words: "Dad? Mum's dead."

SCAB!

Who never fights for his rights
    but reaps all the benefits
And for his fellow workers never gives two shits?

Thinks the boss' hot air will keep him warm and fine
And scoffs at the strikers freezing on the picket line?

Who's got a mortgage, car, season ticket,
    timeshare in Corfu
But can't spare a couple of quid for his weekly
    union dues?

Brown-nosing managers,
    tongue wedged up their cracks
Convinced he'll be spared
    from those destined to be sacked.

Who's got pension, holiday/sick pay, paternity leave
That was won by the union he betrays and deceives?

Prejudice reinforced by scum rag unfit for arse
In his fitted turncoat, a traitor to his class –
SCAB!

SECONDS OUT

When I wore black
I was parading a lack,
And a lass would pass,
Place her face in a book
Or sadly shook
At the barking sap
Hammered by attack,
Shooting off his mouth,
Stabbing himself in the back.
Advertising
No surprise in
A void devoid of colour;
What could be duller
Than a whole portfolio
Of the lies
Of denial?
Count up the debts
On my dead cigarettes,
In the pails of chewed nails,
In the lines in the sand in my hand –
In my hand 'cross my face,
Down the sides,
Ghost train rides
Moodswings and slides
Away, confides
To the brides,
The jilted brides,
The rigid, frigid brides I get.

But today the sky is grey,
But, hey, let it roll away.
The sun's back from the mender
And will shine in all its splendour.
Need I ask to bask in the hue-myriad glory?
See my pain go with each cup of rainbow tea
you pour me.
You floor me.

SHARK

I'm throwing my work shoes in the river.
I'm exchanging cold metal for hot smoke.
No more paper to meticulously misdeliver.
I'll vegetate and meet a series of cosmic jokes.
I'll compose a symphony for police sirens
And open a gallery with no floors or walls.
I'll grow a hairstyle like Lord Byron's
And talk balls.

I make enemies to stave off the boredom.
I'll get drunk on the red-faced tears they cry.
I've got the best friends because I can afford them.
When the cash runs out, so do they – Tatty-bye!
I've got a little plane that I privately flew out
To my desert island where I find a shark on the dunes.
With his last dying breath he spews out
My work shoes.

SHARKEY'S MACHINE

Fuck you, Edith Piaf,
I got regrets by the score,
Like the time I dropped my drawers
For that one jaw-dropping whore.
She forgot to torch the evidence
And didn't delete the files.
Now her old man's on my tail
And he's eating up the miles.

Bitch is hitched to an ass-hat:
Psympleton Psycho Pseth.
So dense he makes his own gravity,
Says the capital of France is F.
She's hotter than Satan's butt-plug
And dirty and obscene.
I came like Niagara
In Sharkey's machine.

Sharkey's machine, Sharkey's machine
Give me the car keys to Sharkey's machine
Between me and freedom is a cavernous ravine
Give me hope and a bag of dope and
    Sharkey's machine.

Making something out of nothing,
A kiss ain't just a kiss.
Must a lifetime of pain cost me
One sinful night of bliss?

Heavenly free love
Comes at a hell of a price.
Maybe "Go fuck yourself"
Is practical advice.

He's got muscles on his muscles
Has Psympleton Psycho Pseth.
He's the meanest recidivist
Who ever punched out breath.
Get a sick note from my mama
And tell it to the marines.
Get behind a wig
In Sharkey's machine.

Sharkey's machine, Sharkey's machine
Give me the car keys to Sharkey's machine
Lady Luck's kicked me in the nuts and
    they're wedged up my spleen
But I'm singing soprano in Sharkey's machine.

Sharkey's machine, Sharkey's machine
Give me the car keys to Sharkey's machine
Lady Luck kicked me in the nuts and
    they're wedged up my spleen
But I got cash in the bank, gas in the tank and
Sharkey's machine.

SOFT AFTERNOONS

On soft afternoons we share
At the pretty, boring glare
Discollapsing, merge in to the chair
Where the yeahs go there, there.
Despair of clubs and hearts, throw your hand,
Discreet nodding off, we over stand.
The days we chain crumble, tumble down hold
Dull echo cocoa goes cold.

On soft afternoons we drift
Like sand, like smoke, we settle and sift
For notes in coats, bare-faced, bereft.
The seams are frayed, the warp and weft,
The shapeless drape, the cramp and dampened pall
Hanging like a murderer in the hall.
Drink up the days, smoke out the nights
Till the dawn crawls yawning round, light

On soft afternoons we stick,
Biting down, down into the quick.
Stuck in web, ebb and flow slows,
Suspended like birds and old clothes.
Appeal withers like a pensioner skin.
No-one hears you screaming deep within.
Elastic gone, unravelling, thought distraught
In soft afternoons we're caught.

SOFT SHOES

I heard you before I saw you
Floorboard creaking as you crushed a roach
Feeling that I'd bore you
I looked down as we approached

I ascended
From the dark damp basement;
I pretended
I knew what claiming my own space meant.
You're coming down
From the moonset shining attic
You're burnt out
Face frozen ... automatic.

And though we were dissimilar
You were strangely familiar
Alarm bells started ringing in my head;
I don't suppose it matters
You have the same suit as me but in tatters
It looked like it was hanging by a thread.

I asked, "Do I know you?
Somehow I think that I do"
And you stared at me, eyes crazed and red
There on the stair.
I heard your words, "Beware,
    Satan wears soft shoes" was all you said.
"Satan wears soft shoes" was all you said.

He heard me before he saw me
Floorboard creaking as I crushed a roach
Guessing he would bore me
I glared at him as we approached.

I descended
Down from the sky-kissed rain-pissed roof
I pretended
To make peace with my fading youth.
He was climbing
Like every civil civilian
With perfect timing
Shuffling to oblivion.

And though we were dissimilar
He was strangely familiar
A memory fighting through mind mist
Had I already lived this scene?
He has the same suit as me but clean
Not frayed at the ankle, neck or wrist

He asked, “Have we met before?
I think so but can’t be sure.”
And I stared at him, eyes crazed and red
There on the stair
I whispered, “Beware,
Satan wears soft shoes” and I fled.
“Satan wears soft shoes” and I fled.

SOMEONE ELSE'S WIFE

You know, it's the ones
Who faced the big guns
Who are most wary to talk of war;
And hear me, Lord above,
The same applies to love
So you see why I can't say much more.

Hair flecked with confetti,
You and him, and I bet he
Relished being the envy of the reception;
And I was the best man
And you know I still am
Though my speech was a triumph of deception.

Wrong place wrong time, too little too late,
Is this the story of my life
Where I'm always someone else's husband
And you're someone else's wife?

When I sigh
And get gazey-eyed
At the kitchen sink doing the dishes,
She doesn't know
(Or, at least, I hope so)
What my aching wish is.

In lieu of sex
I send you texts
Short and sweet and cryptic;

And instead of dirt
I'm scrubbing from my shirt
I wish it was your lipstick.

Wrong place wrong time, too little too late,
Is this the story of my life
Where I'm always someone else's husband
And you're someone else's wife?

We've hard-learned
Everybody gets burned
And we could've been the perfect match;
If we could break these chains
I'd be kissing your veins
And you can rub my paunch or bald patch.

Can we ever be
Together and free
Not have to listen for a key in the door,
Or could this feeling so strong
Transpire to be wrong
And we're left with nothing at all to say in the morning?

I'll never know, it's the end of the show
Of the story of my life;
I'm always someone else's husband
You're always someone else's wife.

SOMEONE'S GOT TO GIVE

Through the hole cut in the fence,
No land of happy accidents.
Scratch the shopping-, waiting-lists;
Resounding screams and pounding fists.
Houses for sale.
Bad news in the mail.
Someone's got to give.

Down the winding village lane
Through ornament-strewn window; pain.
Quiet lives like candles snuffed
By the hand of injustice rough.
Gardens need doing.
Cups of tea are stewing.
Someone's got to give.

The urgency for things they wished
Are suddenly extinguished;
The wallpaper, the holiday,
Go with them into the clay.
Homework unwritten,
The pair of winter mittens
No-one needs to give.

In the House they demand the facts,
And shout about the nut that cracked.
But there's no hero, no villain;
Whitehaven, Dunblane, Enniskillen.

It’s so hard to make it.
In the end you can’t take it.
And someone’s got to give.

TALKING 'BOUT MY GENITALIA

Whole world exploding at the seams
But let's all focus on what's in my jeans
Don't wanna discuss society's failure
I'm talking about my genitalia

I want everyone to be totally free
To shut their traps and pay attention to me
Black cab or Hitler, I won't hail you
Too busy talking 'bout my genitalia

All you starving, tortured refugees
None of you suffer as bad as me
Straight innocent jailed? I won't bail you
Cos you don't care about my genitalia

I'm an upstanding member
Of a screwed society,
I get in a flap or out a hole
But always consensually.
Traumatised is normalised
Keep up with the downs;
Pillowcases hide red faces
Riding with the Ku Klux Klowns.

TATTOO REMOVAL SERVICE

Gwyneth, I think of you but, admittedly, not often
And over time my ardour has softened
And with memories edited carefully
I'll make a laugh riot from our non-event of
 the century.
Cut free from the vine, afternooning in my bedroom
I was an idiot, yes, but an idiot for you;
My fingers twirling your curling rusty hair,
 I was smitten
For you I'd paint my bollocks blue and hop nude to
 Thames Ditton.
But beyond exploratory kisses and
 tentative caresses
We never divested ourselves of trousers and dresses
Drinking in your red acne, black eyeliner,
 chapped lips
Hungry for what lay midpoint 'neath your hips.
I was hampered by a weird fear, cripplingly shy
And tongue-tied as you rhapsodised about
 some other guy
Dying inside, your joy for that boy had me furious
And yet I did nothing, said less,
 and of me you were incurious.
Fast forward a few Whitsuns
 and up the aisle you trudged
Hitching to a slug who turned
 your dream palace into sludge
You deserved better than a life of monotony

You were a sweetheart, Gwyn,
even though it didn't beat for me.

But why am I pinning the blame on him
and letting you off scot free?
We never were an item – 'cept in my dreams –
so he never stole you from me
No black-tashed villain,
he was just your average normal bloke
Perhaps fat cocks and throbbing wallets
were enough to make you soak.
Or maybe it was cosmic boredom or existential crisis
That Hyde and Jekyll'd you from vodka bingeing
to yoga and dance classes
Whiteflagging to white rum,
red wine and blue moods
Swinging with a sucker around your
mortgaged mortuary living room.
No, Gwyn, I'm not face down scoffing from
a nosebag of regret
I've smoked down and stubbed out
carnal desire's cigarette
And if we met again would I feel any pain
If you crinkled your brow and asked me my name?
And in your diary discover that I was at most
a margin jotting
A footnote, a sideline, a doodle, a poodle,
a smudged ink blotting?

Did you find the best way to survive
    was by getting numb and dumber
In your purse is there a card with the
    Tattoo Removal Service's number?

TATTOO REMOVAL SERVICE (Radio Jingle)

Your favourite football team failing to score?
Your pop star pin-up a convicted child molester?
Your ex-sweetheart leaving a foul taste?
Call the Tattoo Removal Service today!

"Call the Tattoo Removal Service
When you don't wish to be reminded
Give us a call, and what it is, we'll find it
And of that ugly vision you'll be blinded.
We'll turn it into a blank canvas;
Call the Tattoo Removal Service."

Terms and conditions apply.

TATTOO REMOVAL SERVICE (TV Advert)

What was once normal is now twice strange
Fresh fruit will perish and stink
Times and minds are subject to change
Break the chains of yesteryear's ink.
Call the Tattoo Removal Service
What you once thought beautiful is now mutilated
The Tattoo Removal Service
In your face the bomb of time has detonated
Tattoo Removal Service
Your body temple needs to be redecorated
The Tattoo Removal Service
Cast off the past and be liberated
Now.

THAT'S ALL WE NEED

I'm a there-found chair-bound
Narrow-mounded stare-hound;
An up-wound downtown
Get a round drink drowned
All-round good eggbound
Yeah sound crowd clown.
The now and then is there and then
And I don't care now.

Oh no, that's all we need,
Another broken-hearted singer.
Put down your guitar, please,
And give us the peace you didn't bring her.

An off-the-peg straight-leg
Trouser browser e-beg
Drip-dry shirt tie
Money crawls, time flies
Credit checks, edit texts
Flat dreg, keg leg
Kerfuffle muffle as I knuckle shuffle
To a bj-peg

Oh no, that's all we need,
Another broken-hearted singer.
He's gonna spill every bean
He's gonna put us through the wringer.

Left at an all-night right-wing
Wingding singsong,
A mink-thonged King Kong
Plays genital ping-pong.
The fame game blame shame
The same lame ding-dong
Thunderin' while I'm wonderin'
How it's all gone wrong.

Oh no, that's all we need,
Another woeful soulful singer.
Don't break my heart, break out the weed,
Get a refund on the flowers you didn't fling her.

THE BANK OF MUM AND DAD

Jeer, jeer, jeer at us ancient coupon clippers
Sneer, sneer, sneer at us unlucky lucky-dippers
We're crossword puzzlers, tea guzzlers,
    sherry sippers
Doorstop sandwich!
Gout bandage!

But when your laughing leaflets are all spent, boy
And your future's blue 'cos
    you ain't got a red cent, boy
There's no need to go bent for the rent, boy
In a rut?
It's a short cut

To the Bank of Mum & Dad
When you're potless in Islamabad
The Bank of Mum & Dad
When you thought you were having it large
    but find you've been had
The Bank of Mum & Dad

When the world grows up around you
    and you're left small
Swallow your pride, make that call
To the Bank of Mum & Dad.

Life is a football and you've got to head it
Yellow brick road paved with gold;
    you've got to tread it

Flash your cash cards with unlimited credit
But when they're cut
Doors are shut

A gentleman's handshake falls off at the wrist
The country club doorman says you're not on the list
And the red carpet rolls up in a blue mist
No bunce to burn?
About-turn

To the Bank of Mum & Dad
Odds bodkins! Egad!
The Bank of Mum & Dad
When your have-it-largesse makes you large-S'd Sad
The Bank of Mum & Dad

Mock us for serenading our falcon
    with a spinet and flute
But you'll be singing our little number
    when you're out of loot
All the way!!

To the Bank of Mum & Dad
Always open!
The Bank of Mum & Dad
24/7!
The Bank of Mum & Dad
No VAT!

The Bank of Mum & Dad
Interest-free!
The Bank of Mum & Dad
Don't declare it!
The Bank of Mum & Dad
Don't you share it!
The Bank of Mum & Dad
Easy terms!
The Bank of Mum & Dad
'Cos you're from the firm!
The Bank of Mum & Dad

THE LAST HELLO

Am I in your dream
Or are you in mine?
Is this where you rise high
And I decline?
Come all this way, so much to say
And nothing to show.
I'm no good at goodbyes;
Let's make this the last hello.

Each tear dries in time
Each flower dies and rots.
You like to drink, so open and sink
A bottle of forget-me-lots.
The way we were's not the way we are,
Love will ebb and flow.
I'm no good at goodbyes;
Make this our last hello.

THE LAST POST

When I land and unwind I'll write her a postcard
Over a black coffee and a Gauloise.
Maybe a saucy cartoon -
    a busty nudist and a coastguard,
Or a scenic one - a church or some bar.

But what can I write after what we've been through?
The coffee chills as I chew my pen.
"Having a great time" is spiteful and patently untrue.
I'm here and now, not there and then.

It's time to draw a line through
    what left us so scarred
And leave point-scoring P.S.'s unread.
I pay my bill and leave, tearing up the tacky postcard
With the inscription "Wish you were dead".

THE LIST OF MR. PFISTER

The list of Mr Pfister
Made no mention of his sister,
Just some ointment for his blister
And "Have the go-go girls come?
Choreograph the stage fights
And don't bring up the house lights,
Get a hammer for the termites
And will someone do their sums?
We need to settle these invoices
Don't defrost the choc-ices
Ensure the wigs go back to Joyce's
And Ted's not too drunk to drive.
Put some fresh soap in the basins,
Replace the defacings,
Get Ted to collect the Masons
And have the go-go girls arrived?

If the host must die, die smiling,
And have the workmen finished tiling?
Has Maureen finished filing?
Is she petrified of hard graft?
Pay off that smart arse comic;
He were bloody chronic.
Was it an act or naturally moronic
Die? I nearly laughed!
And put the Siamese twins on half wages
And the tigers in their cages.
It was plain outrageous
To let them out in the interval."

The list of Mr Pfister
Made no mention of his sister
But re: the go-go girls was most insistent
When they're here to call.

THE MED MEN

Come on, hand out the beta-blockers
To the heaven's door knockers
Sagging in God's waiting room;
Another hour, another pill,
Push my wheelchair up the hill
And point my ear trumpet at The Goons.

All alone, we never walk,
Kneecaps crumble like chalk,
Sweating bullets turning the handle on the door;
Blood thicker than molasses,
Hanging on for our freedom passes,
That's what we're all dying for.

I shit blood and piss pus in the lavatory
And my bones crack like double-time
in a castanet-testing factory.

We're the med men,
Got no hair, ain't got a prayer,
The chemist's our only friend.
We're the med men,
Going off in an ambulance,
Ain't coming back again.

No, there's no point in your betting
You won't be a bedwetting cretin.
The odds on decay are steeply stacked;

Haphazardly shaved and half-dressed,
A rank, damp stench and depressed
'Cos your anti-depressants made you fat.

And what's that between your
withered and veiny legs?
A slumbering slug and two mouldy Scotch eggs.

We're the med men,
Got no hair, ain't got a prayer,
The chemist's our only friend.
We're the med men,
Going off in an ambulance,
Ain't coming back again.

THE POINT OF LIGHT

It's not the pall of smoke
That hangs beneath the ceiling
Or the spill of drink
That fails to kill the feeling.
It's not the calls to friends
I make to diminish your importance
Or our own conversations
That now reduce me to silence.
It's the time and distance
Between what we say and mean;
Growing older, getting colder,
Freezing a perfect summer scene
Which appears again to scold me in a winter night -
Why, too late, can I see the point of light?

It's not my jealousy
And reading your letters and diaries.
Knowledge isn't love,
It's possession and my relentless inquiries
Picked apart the bonds
Accusing you of crimes not committed,
And your testimony
Was not accepted or permitted.
I was stupid and brutal,
More than beasts locked in dark cages,
A heart as black as ink,
Please someone tear out and burn these pages.

In the flames, I'd see again
your smile kind and bright -
Why, too late, can I see the point of light?

It's not a pot of gold
For me awaiting on the horizon.
It's not your kiss of forgiveness, either,
And that's not surprising.
I'll get what I deserve
And I expect nothing less,
And if I learn my lesson -
Well, that's anybody's guess.
Shoot the sun out of the sky,
It's only energy wasted.
There's nothing left for me to see;
Your beauty - I defaced it.
Draw the blinds on tomorrow,
damn me to eternal night -
Why, too late, can I see the point of light?

THE SMILES

Making a secret wish
Blowing dandelion clocks.
Smoke my first cigarette
Hidden in my sandwich box.
Our blanket is my duffel coat.
Later we'll sail paper boats –
Ten to one, mine won't float;
I've got clumsy fingers
And my hayfever lingers.

It was you
Who
Put
The smiles on me.

This flower beneath your chin
Will tell if you like butter.
When you ease me your lazy grin
I lose my schoolboy stutter.
Laying watching clouds drift by,
Our hands will shade our eyes.
We sit up at a sound nearby;
It's the butterfly collectors,
They'll not disturb or affect us.

It was you
Who
Put
The smiles on me

A spin on the roundabout
Then a go on the see-saw.
The sun sinks behind the factory.
Our mums are calling us indoors.
Summer scrams like a gang of thieves.
I'll watch the bonfire of dead autumn leaves.
I'll look at lovehearts on the trees.
If I don't see you December
I'll always remember

It was you
Who
Put
The smiles on me

THE SORE THUMB PARADE

The tartan brothel creepers
    with the three inch tread,
The hairy yeti jacket, zero street cred,
The heavy-brocade wine red waistcoat
    (Camden market),
The retro-modernist jacket with obligatory target,
The crimson winkle pickers
    that bore a faint cheese fragrance,
The scuffed, faded espadrilles –
    heirlooms of vagrants?
The Fabrizio red raincoat right from Prague
    left in my closet;
It was bold but plain but stylish – like you. Or was it?
Take it away, boys, take it away.

The brown suede cowboy boots you left
    for me to trip over in the hall,
The Swiss Air t-shirt you got in Madrid
    when our luggage was in Nepal,
Hankies, hankies, so many hankies,
    plain, patterned, gingham,
And your Vivienne Westwood bag fetish,
    you could never fling 'em,
The black cashmere cardigan that,
    when you sat down, rode up,
The heavy slate grey trews from Toast
    that could not fold up,
The low-cut Zara pink-and-white dress
    that exposed your Bingo wings,

The unopened packets of black hold-ups –
    the box of sovereign rings:
Take it away, boys, take it away.

Prolonged exposure to direct sunlight
Will cause synthetics to fade
As will the days of our crazy phase
As King and Queen of the Sore Thumb Parade.

The chunky Rothko leg-warmers
    knitted by your mum,
The pale blue cardigan that still smells of cum,
Your Bio-Oil for scarred, stretched, dehydrated skin,
Your Aloe Calming Facial Cleanser
    for 'party' and sensitive skin,
Your Camomile Gentle Eye make-up remover,
Your soya-based burn and inflammation soother:
Take it away, boys, take it away.

THE UNINVITED GUEST

When I walk in the park I stop photosynthesis,
When I talk all you think is "Halitosis",
The modern day Samuel Johnsons
    rip me out their diaries,
Professional wasters book themselves into
    The Priory.

The good times find the clock has stopped
    the second I arrive,
The pro-life lobby's popularity takes a nose-dive,
My threadbare yarns are ripe
    for cloth-ears' unpicking
And pacifists line up to give me a royal kicking.

I'm the flapping fly vomiting in your caviar,
I make Alcoholics Anonymous make a bee-line
    for the bar,
Razor-sharp witlings quickly cut their throats,
Even the most stoic waiters hurry for their coats.

I pose for an artist and he tears out his eyes.
The Worst Dressed Man hands me his
    treasured prize.
The bent went straight and ladies turn lesbian.
The internet goes stone dead the second I log in.

I'm the flapping fly vomiting in your caviar,
I make Alcoholics Anonymous make a bee-line
    for the bar.

Go to all points North, South, East and West;
In the wide world party I'm the uninvited guest.

THE UP SET

If you're feeling post-dated
Ill-fated, isolated
There's a niche clique
That'll make you feel unique:
The Up Set

If the new makes you wary
And changes strike you scary
The situation's not doomed
You can find room in
The Up Set

The Up Set
(We look after our own)
The Up Set
(Reject the strange and unknown)
The Up Set
(Think with a megaphone)
The Up Set

Let's put an end to taxes
The rich must be rewarded
Punish the poor, let them starve
If they can't afford it.
Prison terms for strikers
Torpedo refugees
I believe in free speech
So long as they agree with me.

The Up Set
(We are the entitled)
The Up Set
(Upholding tradition is vital)
The Up Set
(Ban films that are subtitled)
The Up Set.

THESE SHOES

I can hear the echo of your footsteps
Fade into obscurity.
I can hear the ring of hollow laughter
That's still surrounding me.

Don't think I'll be complaining
When you don't answer my call.
Don't think I'll be crying
When you pass me by in the hall.
It's just a bit of dust
In my eye, that's all,
And these shoes ain't going nowhere.

I can see the place is in the distance
Where we both once tried to live.
I can see a face stare back in the mirror
And he asks, "Who's that you're with?"

I tell myself it's no-one
And all my money's spent.
I look at our initials
That we carved in wet cement.
It's reassuring that they're still here
Although you went,
And these shoes ain't going nowhere.

I can touch the secret diaries of reminiscence
And I'm haunted by the ghost of truth.
I can touch these four walls we kept ourselves in
But it's too late to touch you.

Don't think I'm going to starve
For lack of breadcrumbs that you throw,
And don't consider for a moment
That you've paid back all you owe,
And don't assume I'm going to be heartbroken
When you go
'Cos these shoes ain't going nowhere.

THEY DON'T NEED ME

Electric's gone and my feet are feeling the cold.
Another empty evening stretches out
And loneliness takes hold.

And my friends are having the time of their lives
And they don't need me.

Everyone's at the party except me.
A big dog won't let me come down
From my tree.

And my friends are having the time of their lives
And they don't need me.

Across the water I can hear their laughter.
I'll be told all the jokes
The morning after.

And my friends are having the time of their lives
And they don't need me.

They say to me, "Oh, man, you should've been there."
Well, I would have if any one of them
Remembered.

And my friends are having the time of their lives
And they don't need me.

THIS IS ALL YOU GET

Kicked-over dustbins
Crunched-up beer cans
Wheezing old men
Stubbing out cigarettes;
This is all you get.
Leak in the ceiling
Punctured football
Holes in your pockets
Plenty of bus tickets;
This is all you get.
War hero pensions
Defaced gravestones
Indoctrination
Cold hard monetarism;
This is all you get.

This is all you get.
This is all that they give you;
A cold, numb, no-hope wasteland
With no way for you to break through
This is all you get.
So what are you going to do?
What are you going to do?

Electric and gas bills
Broken telly
Shit on the radio
Mum sold the stereo;
This is all you get.

Yesterday's paper
Housewife coughing
Missing your girlfriend
Playing scratched records;
This is all you get.
Watching the news
Brainwash dead-end
Finding school photos
Of friends you've forgotten;
This is all you get.

This is all you get.
This is all that they give you;
A cold, numb, no-hope wasteland
With no way for you to break through
This is all you get.
So what are you going to do?
What are you going to do?

TWO CAMELS

Englishman on camel,
Destination Cairo.
Leaving Casablanca
Four thousand miles to go.
Thunderbox, moustache net
Amongst his cargo;
Englishman on camel
Leaving Morocco.

Second Englishman on camel,
British outpost in Cairo.
Heading for Morocco,
Pints of perspiration flow.
Led by sextant and compass,
He's going solo;
Englishman on camel
With bout of lumbago.

Englishmen on camels,
Little do they know
They will pass at a wadi
Near Zeralda-Boudouaou.
Will they greet the other?
Will they exchange info
When they meet each other
Toe to camel toe?

Two thousand miles of desert,
Water running low,
Dust mouth 'neath solar topee
And free-standing parasol.
Oasis was a mirage,
Scorching sandstorm blow.
Spot move on horizon
Warped in heatwave glow.

A quarter mile between them,
Englishmen don't know
If the nearing figure
Is a friend or foe.
Space shrink in-between them,
Anticipation grow,
Features become more distinct,
Eyes strain in heat haze glow.
They're level with each other,
Looking down their nose:
Is he out of Sandhurst?
Is he Eton or Harrow?
Beneath chinless faces,
MCC ties show,
So both men tip their topees
And politely say, "What ho!"

W.A.S.P. IN W.E.B.

White Anglo-Saxon Protestant
In West End bar
She came down on me like an ounce of bricks
In transparent camouflage.
Effortlessly pulling me
She's pushing an open door
In the days of rock'n'Rollerball
A road apple rolling 'cross the floor.

She's a star not twinkling in the firmaments of
Liza and Dino.
Raze I.Q., raise skirt and shoe to become slum extra
Incognito.
Just another anorexic sex tourist with an
Inflamed libido;
A long-term lovesick outpatient dope hoping to
overdose
On your placebo.

Picking at the fabric
Of her red wig *char-rack-tah*
Checked in as Laura Kenyon
Decked in Charlie and Max Factor.
Was it in a dream I seen her
Gurning at the Grammys
From my sweat-soaked hospital bed
In my sweet-stained 'jammies?
My drip was saline
Her dress was A-line

And now she's making a bee-line
To me like a feline
Preying on a lark.
She's mentally kicking my tyres
Checking my gear and exhaust and seein'
If I cruise with the choirs.
You can't beat addiction
It's the white, the green or the brown.
I used to light a candle for good luck
Till my house burnt down.
We shared all her cigarettes,
Small talk, tall tales and fables;
How I pledged my love to my school girlfriend
Till the end of timetables.
She said, "You English hide behind jokes
And artists lie to their friends
And confess all to total strangers"
And I said, "Good to see you again!"
The room was getting tighter
It was hard to easy speak
So we shuffled amidst the kerfuffle
Dancing chic to Chic.
White Anglo-Saxon protest singer
Slumming unconvincingly
Am-dram no-thank-you-ma'am
Bumming fags mincingly.

I won't let failure go to my head
I knew I was her splash and dash
For her to turn it into an after-dinner joke
For her to turn it into song and cash.
Pale blue kitchen morning after
Desire and drugs worn off
Bad skin, bad breath, silence broken
By a duet for smokers' cough.
Lower than an ant's spats
I made her *erf scram-blade*
Then exit, this cheap thrillionaire
Who's been bought, owned and played...

WATER DUCK BACK

Come on, you finger-waggers,
    you naggers and you slaggers
Water duck back, water duck back
Ridicule me, you giggling gaggers,
    dress me head to foot in daggers
Water duck back, water duck back

In the human race, you're a non-starter
Get up, get out, get happy, get Carter
When you shut up the world gets 10% smarter.

All you phoney moany groaners,
    you stickers and you stoners
Water duck back, water duck back
All your heads are solid boners;
    a drone of brain donors
Water duck back, water duck back

I tell a joke and I'm accused of stealing it off Jim
Get your facts straight, dimwit,
    I'm the one who told him!

Bottle clinkers, IQ shrinkers,
    single out joined-up thinkers,
Water duck back, water duck back
Dressed up in your blinkers, do I give a tinker's?
Water duck back, water duck back

You'll find when you find something to place belief in
There's an army of boots racing to kick your teeth in.

Water duck back, water duck back

WE'RE BACK

WE'RE BACK! – reunited and reformed
WE'RE BACK! – unrepentant, unconformed
WE'RE BACK! – it's like we've never been away
WE'RE BACK! – playing the sounds of yesterday
today!
WE'RE BACK!

Cue World Exclusive features
In every magazine,
Forums discuss our lyrics
Trying to work out what they mean.
You're more than fans to us, you're family,
And it's great seeing you all again
Waiting for nine hours in Hyde Park
In torrential wind and rain.

'Cos WE'RE BACK! – reunited and reformed
WE'RE BACK! – taking nostalgia by storm
WE'RE BACK! – to shake our fists at The Man
WE'RE BACK! – don't forget to visit our merch stand
WE'RE BACK!

Photos scrutinised, 'shopped and vetted,
Moody lighting, in long shot
'Cos worse than a baby born dead with AIDS
Is a pop star with a bald spot.
Our entourage this time round
Includes the wives and kids.

No chance of a hotel roasting,
We're being watched like invalids

'Cos – WE'RE BACK!

We're gonna play our biggest album
In its entirety –
Even the bassist's crap solo track
'Cos he needs the royalties.
Film it to preserve the memory,
Re-record the bum notes for the DVD,
A world premiere on the BBC
Introduced by Paul Gambaccini.
We're all right, Jack –
Yeah, we're back!

Like you, the drummer's out of time
And the singer's voice is shot,
But you've got to love us
Because we're all you've got.
Of course this ain't a last chance rip-off –
We're doing it all for you,
So come and re-live the virginity you lost
In a club in '92.
Our back catalogue was an impassioned scream,
The wild yell of rebel youth;
Now it sounds like an old fart
Who has trouble chewing soup.

Old men spouting young men's words?
It's surreal, hard to understand.
I can't explain so fuck it,
EVERYBODY CLAP YOUR HANDS!

'Cos - WE'RE BACK! - the critics all agree
WE'RE BACK! - five star reviews guaranteed
WE'RE BACK! - we're in this together, you and me
WE'RE BACK! - tied to rock mythology
WE'RE BACK!

WHAT HAPPENED?

THE FIRST MANAGER:
"Who was it who praised you to the skies
When you were barely mediocre?
Who was it who left you with the right guys –
The dealers and the smokers?
Who stayed up for three nights running,
Setting up your website and Facebook page?
Who was it who fed you quotes so stunning
Stephen Fry fell off the stage?

Oh well, I'll give you three guesses
    if you can't remember,
But you're living it up in your private club
    and I'm not a member.
What happened to the friend I had?
What happened?
What happened to the friend I had?

Who was it who got you on the A-list
Rubbing shoulders with Noel at the bar?
Who ensured the paparazzi never missed
You stepping out of a car?
Who was it who paid for your Hoxton flat
And your studio space?
Who was it who cleaned up your act
And airbrushed your face?

Well, your P.A. says you can't see me now,
    you're so frightfully busy,
And she's got to go – 'Jarvis is on the line' –
    and I wonder, 'Is he?'

What happened to the friend I had?
What happened?
What happened to the friend I had?"

THE ARTIST:
"Yes, I know who plucked me from obscurity
And spread me over the front pages,
Who made me an object of curiosity
Where everything I say and do is 'Outrageous!'
Who made it impossible for me to step outdoors
Without strangers being cruel and hateful,
Shouting 'We hate you', 'Sell-out!' and 'Filthy whore';
I'm sorry – do I sound ungrateful?

Well, I could tell you all about my new life in Hell
But you'd only call up the papers with an exclusive
    to sell.

What happened to the friend I had?
What happened?
What happened to the friend I had?"

WHATEVER HAPPENED TO PHILIP FORD?

Was he sighted in a Hong Kong bar
Arm-wrestling a one-eyed cripple?
Was that him in Piccadilly Circus in '91
Sucking Eros' nipple?
It's said he's over 30 stone,
Addicted to Jelly Tots.
Others maintain he's off the coast of Spain
Hiring out a fleet of yachts.

Let's have a look at the old scoreboard
In the out-house by Deryck Guyler's washboard.
Anyone here seen King Arthur's sword?
And whatever happened to Philip Ford?

Could he be an eco-warrior
In the Amazon saving trees,
Or a Berkeley Square car dealer
Handing over log book and keys?
Maybe he's a waiter at The Dorchester
Handy with menus and cruets,
Or the owner of a village sweet shop,
Dentures stained by cigs and Chew-Its.

Have all the Double Diamonds been poured?
When did all the jewels in the crown become flawed?
How many goals has Bobby Moore scored?
And whatever happened to Philip Ford?

Is he a silk rober, calm and sober
Or completely out of his tree?
In a free state, does he contemplate
Whatever happened to me?

Maybe he couldn't handle it,
Lost his job, wife, home and mind.
Maybe he got ground down
By the daily grind.
Maybe he's living rough on the streets,
The once laughing eyes now hidden.
I often think of Philip Ford
And I sometimes wish I didn't.

When did the last train guard shout "All aboard"?
What was the last Tarantino film you endured?
Who was the last sex symbol you adored?
And whatever happened to Philip Ford?

WONDERWORLD

The dawn is breaking
And I awaken,
Rubbing the sleep from my dreamy eyes.
The dewdrops glisten
And I listen
To birdsong carried on the lightening skies.

Hair is combed,
Teeth are brushed,
Sleepyheads are being rushed
To find their place in the crush
Of trains and cars and buses.
I wonder what the fuss is
In my big warm bed so snug and tightly curled;
In my wonderworld.

I hear car doors slamming,
Cursing and damning;
The Monday-Friday chorus chimes bang on time.
Housewives complaining,
"It's started raining.
Hurry, get the washing off the line."

Pots to wash,
Plates as well,
Bin the bread crust and eggshell,
Fix the ornament that fell
During a game of kiss chase –

I still feel the kiss on my face,
Warm as the sun that glowed and swirled
Over my wonderworld.

Workers returning,
Streetlights burning,
Sister Luna pulls her dark duvet on the day.
Fill the slippers,
Grill the kippers,
Let the stereotyping pool drain away.

Slip off guard,
Go cold stream,
You're lit by a flickering screen.
Drift in and out of a close-of-daydream,
No care where the next hit comes from –
Schoolboy blade, madman bullet,
    governmental bomb.
Take shelter where no hate missile can be hurled;
My wonderworld.

YOU DON'T GET ME

You get theoretical,
You get how e is mc squared.
You get strategical,
You get how he who had won had dared.
You get numerical,
You get 2 4 1, nought-y.
You get alphabetical,
You get Y I H U, O G.

You get the tree of life, its branches of philosophy;
You get Adam, you get Eve, but you don't get me.

You get complimentary,
You get words worth their weight in gold.
You get documentary,
You get how each life dies to be told.
You get commentary,
You get looking up and down the knows.
You get inventory,
You get labelled like meat or clothes.

You get time, you get space,
    you get your name and face in history;
You get three wishes,
    but it's so vicious that you don't get me.

You get malls, you get calls,
    you get Peters to pay Pauls,

You get Marx, you get god,
    you get work, you get odd,
You get min, you get max,
    you get ticks, you get tax,
You get in, you get out,
    you get stuff, you get nowt,
You get sick, you get votes,
    you get woe, you get jokes,
You get cold, you get cough,
    you get on, you get off!

CREDITS

All songwords composed by Paul Hamilton, except for:

'Excellenté Presidenté': written by Paul Hamilton
with contributions by Andy Thomson.
Song title by Dave Toynton.

'Best': written by Paul Hamilton, edited and arranged by Andy Thomson.

'Four Chords And A Capo': Original song and concept by Dave Pope. This is an unused version by Paul Hamilton, retaining only the title, the mention of the Highway Code and the line "Click-track, I lean back, set the tone dirty and rough" from Pope's original lyric.

'Half-Life', 'I.C.U.' and 'Old Dog': written by Paul Hamilton, edited and arranged by Dave Pope.

'Sharkey's Machine': written by Paul Hamilton,
edited by Doug Murphy.

NOTES

'168' refers to my initials – P being the 16th letter of the alphabet, H the eighth.

'Best' is narrated by George Best.

'Do It Myself': 'Calibre' is deliberately mispronounced to rhyme with 'fibre'. It's a Tony Hancock thing.

'Featherstonehaugh, Featherstonehaugh, Wriothesley' is pronounced 'Fanshawe, Fanshawe, Rocksley'.

'IVY' is pronounced 'For Y'. Y is Yossarian, the character from the Joseph Heller novel *Catch-22*.

'Kolibri' is narrated by Joseph Goebbels.

As of July 2024, 'Med Men', 'Meningitis' and 'Old Dog' are unrecorded.

SMOKING ANT RECORDS

DISCOGRAPHY

Most of the following recordings can be found at
https://bisonics.bandcamp.com/music

Note: Songs marked with an asterisk (*) are *not* written or co-written by PH. Song titles **in bold** indicate songwords included in this volume.

HORRIBLE HEAD *The Gloom of Youth*

[CD / BITE6 / 2010]

Another Fine Mess* **/ I'm A Loser** / Here Comes Edward* / Torn In Two / Got To Get Out* **/ They Don't Need Me** – Another Lonely Place* / Mary Jane / Black Day* / Helping Hand / Live On Lies / New World* / On To A Good Thing* / Wet Weekend / Sinking Slowly / Trojan Horse.

Phil Ford – vocals; Dave Pope – guitar, vocals; Sean Hyde – bass, backing vocals, recording engineer: Paul Hamilton – drums.
All songs taped on a 4-track Portastudio in various Portsmouth living rooms, Spring and Summer 1986. CD credits: Digitized, mixed and mastered by Jason Emberton. Photography by Mark Bleakley. Cover designed by Stephanie Johnson. Produced by Paul Hamilton.

HORRIBLE HEAD *Guillotine Beat*

[Live recording 1986, with 'bonus' studio 1985 songs. Released online / BYTE27 / 2020]

Live in Kingston, 1986: Introduction by BIG BOF* / Got To Get Out* / Wet Weekend / Bitter End / Black Day* **/ This Is All You Get / They Don't Need Me / Pretend** / Sinking Slowly / Another Fine Mess* / Here Comes Edward* / Walking On Sunshine* / Mary Jane / Goodnight From Me*.
Studio, 1985: **This Is All You Get** / I Don't Know / Bitter End – Young Conservatives / Guilty Conscience* **/ Pretend / Not Your Property** / She's Got Teeth*.
Live in Portsmouth, 1986: **Black And White Lines /** Young Conservatives.

Phil Ford – vocal; Dave Pope – guitar, vocal; Sean Hyde – bass, backing vocal; Paul Hamilton – drums. Plus BIG BOF – introduction. Tracks 1–14. Recorded by John Hasket (gracias, amigo) at The Swan in Kingston, 22nd June 1986. Soundboard tape digitised by Emberton, 2010.
Tracks 15–22. Recorded by Steve Hoff at Crystal Rooms, Fratton on 28th November 1985. Live, no overdubs. As if you couldn't tell.
Tracks 23–24. Recorded by Hippy Tosser at Portsmouth Polytechnic All Day Jam, 5th March 1986.
Sleeve design: PH. Produced by PH.

RETICENTS *Grasshopper*

[CD / no catalogue number / 2006]

I Protest* – **Happy Birthday To You** / This Town Is Nowhere / Party Politics / V / Banjo Strummer / Bulletproof* / The Blue Lagoon / **Moon Rising Over London.**

Andy Thomson – guitar, vocal (1, 5, 7, 8), triangle on 'V'. Dave Toynton – bass, ukulele (6), guitar (2). Paul Hamilton – percussion, vocal (2-6, 9).Backing vocals on 'I Protest' by The Perry Hillbillies (Gemma Gayner, ROBBO! Hamilton, Rachael Field, Becky, Chloe, Reticents). Sleeve design: Rachael Field. Produced by Malcolm Gayner.

RETICENTS *Ojimaflips*

[CD / no catalogue number / 2007]

Best / These Shoes / I Can't Help Thinking* / Bee-sting Lips / Old Timers' Disease / Leave Things Alone* / **Excellenté, Presidenté** / Sunshiner / The Long Haul / The State We're In / The Bullshitters' Convention* / The Jokers.

Andy Thomson – guitar, vocals. Dave Toynton – bass, ukulele (5), guitar (8). Paul Hamilton – drums, percussion, vocals. Gavin Murphy – guitar (2, 4), backing vocal (11). Gemma Cummings – vocal (9). Simon Baines – ukulele (8). Sleeve design: Rachael Field. Produced by PH, Malcolm Gayner, Andy Thomson.

RETICENTS *Bad Line*

[CD / no catalogue number / 2008]

If Only We Could* / Nothing Personal / Hall Of Blame / Blue Shirt / I Got You All Wrong* / **Carrier Bags** / Who Needs Luck?* / Missing Person / I'll Dial For You / They Died With Their Phones On.

Andy Thomson – bass, guitars, vocals, piano (8). Gavin Murphy – guitars (2, 5, 6, 7, 8, 10). PH – drums, vocals, percussion, bass (9), loops. Sleeve: Karen Birch. Produced by Malcolm Gayner with Simon Baines.

RETICENTS *I'm All Right*

[CD single / "A Small World Record - SW1" / 2009]

I'm All Right (It's the Others)* / Superwaster / Termites And Tesco's.

Andy Thomson - guitar, vocals. Dave Toynton - bass. PH - drums, vocals, kazoo. Sleeve: >>fwd [a.k.a. Rachael Field]. Produced by Reticents [a.k.a. PH, Thomson].

RETICENTS *I Want One Too*

[download EP / no catalogue number / 2010]

I Want One Too / **In Someone's Hands** / Supersillyass / John Peel.

PH - drums, percussion, vocals, Stylophone. Dave Toynton - bass, guitars, ukulele. Andy Thomson - guitar (1). Jason Emberton: bass and piano (2). Original artwork: Stephanie Johnson. Download artwork: Dave Pope. Recorded by Emberton. Produced by Reticents [a.k.a. PH].

BISONICS *Play For Today*

[CD / BITE1 / 2010]

What Happened / **The Last Post** / Next Door Neighbours / **The List Of Mr. Pfister** / **Bland Foundation** / Tender / Mercenary / W.O.E. / Starecase* / this is / Black Box Recorder / **Someone Else's Wife** / **Beyond** / **The Smiles.** CD hidden tracks [not available on the download version]: I Hate Blues* / Old Hat (78rpm) / When I Am / **Drinking With Jesus** / Yellow (Parts 1-4)*.

Simon Beacon - keyboards, vocals, sax, drums (4). Doug Murphy - guitars, bass, vocals. PH - drums, percussion, vocals. Nick Shaikh - piano (1). Dennis Murphy - keyboard (3). Sleeve drawings: Edward Ward. Design: Stephanie Johnson. Mixed by Malcolm Gayner and Simon Beacon. Produced by Bisonics.

LOUDSNEAKERS *undoneup*

[CD / BITE5 / 2010]

Me And the Moon / Where We Were / Girl On The Bookcase / There Were Tears* / Sorry / Where Did The Love Go? / Nobody Like You / Still Running* / Shut Up Shop.

Sean Hyde - vocals, guitars, bass, mandolin, percussion. Mark Wallis - guitars, harmonica, backing vocals. Kim Ono [a.k.a PH] - drums, percussion. Arthur Higgins - saxophones. Molly & Bethany Hyde - backing vocals ('Nobody Like You'). Ernest Bothershops [a.k.a PH] - inner voice ('There Were Tears'). Sleeve design: Stephanie Johnson. Bag men: Andy 'The Hat' Thomson, Paul 'The Trousers' Hamilton. Produced by Sean Hyde.

DOUG MURPHY + PAUL HAMILTON
Only Two Can Play
[CD / BITE7 / 2011]
Mr Potter Of Creep St. / A Man For All Treasons / The Uninvited Guest / 168 / Someone's Got To Give / I Was Happy Here / Special / **No Father, No Son /** The Ancient Britons.
Doug Murphy - guitars, bass, backing vocals. PH - drums, percussion, vocals, Stylophone. Jason Emberton - keyboards (4, 9). Sleeve: Stephanie Johnson. Mixed by Emberton. Produced by Hamilton & Murphy.

BISONICS *Seconds*
[CD / BITE8 / 2011]
Invitation To A Beheading / A Karaoke Version Of Myself / My Drugly Past (Part 1) / **The Sore Thumb Parade / Shark / Salmon Pink Raincoat** / Five Little Monkeys / **My Drugly Past (Part 2)** / The Block / **Re: Union / Keeping Mum** / Looking For Carl La Fong / **Soft Afternoons** / Broken Pencil / **Seconds Out**.
Doug Murphy - guitars, bass, keyboards, backing vocals. Si Beex - keyboards, effects. PH - drums, vocals, percussion, xylophone (12). Dennis Murphy (guitar solo, 9). Jesper Murphy (guitar solo, 8). Anne Antonsen, Astrid Brunvatne, Åsmund & Toralf Geitung (backing vocals, 12).Recorded at Gamle Slakthuset, Haugesund & Torvastad Kulturhuset, Karmøy, Norway. Engineered by Bjørn Fløystad & Doug Murphy. Sound supervised by Jason Emberton & Si Beex. Sleeve design & CD booklet artwork by Stephanie Johnson. Produced by BISONICS.

JAZZ CATTLE *Relaxing At Gunpoint*

[CD / BITE10 / 2012]

Waves Of Words / **Monsters Must Be Destroyed / Let Me Paint A Picture For You / Kolibri / Wonderworld /** Fuck Cops / **British Empire State / Old Bag** / Dementia-cha-cha / I Came Round.

Andrew Petrie – guitars, keyboards, bass, percussion, sax, clarinet, autoharp, dulcimer (probably), whistle, kazoo, sitar, samples, kitchen sink. PH – voice, one finger-click (British Empire State). Jason Emberton – piano (Wonderworld), pre-production, vocal recordings and mastering. Stephen Morphet – mix and additional recording. Sleeve design: Dave Pope. Our Man In Ascot: Andy 'Topper' Thomson. Produced by Andrew Petrie.

DOUG MURPHY + PAUL HAMILTON *Big Bun*

[download / no catalogue number / 2013]

Godfly / **I Work In A Shop** / Missed Aches / Before The Storm / **The Point Of Light** / Tracer / R U O.K? / Jack's Return Home / **Keeps / Fishes.**

Doug Murphy: bass, guitars, keyboards, vocals. PH: drums, vocals, percussion. PLUS! Jason Emberton – piano ('Fishes', 'The Point Of Light'). Recorded at Westbourne Rehearsal Studios, Bourne Terrace, London W2 between November 2012 and March 2013. Engineered, mixed, edited and mastered by Jason Emberton. Overdougs recorded by Doug Murphy at home in Haugesund, Norway.Cover painting: Gillian Golding. Album title: Gary Page. Download booklet design, layout and graphics: Dave Pope. Executive producer: Andy Thomson. Produced by Hamilton and Murphy.

DOUG MURPHY + PAUL HAMILTON *Two Camels*

[download / no catalogue number / 2013]

Two Camels

DM – Three bass guitars, acoustic guitar, backing vocal. PH – Drums, lead vocal, shells, triangle, temple block, tambourine, tin cans. Recorded at Westbourne Rehearsal Studios, Bourne Terrace, London W2. Jason Emberton: Morocco street recordist, engineer, mixer and masterer. Sleeve design: Dave Pope. Original photography: Hilde Øygarden. Produced by Hamilton & Murphy.

YELLOWJACK *Godot Woz Ere*

[CD / BITE12 / 2014]

We're Back / Half-Life / You Can't Have It **/ Everyone Likes This / Join The Queue / It's Time I Went Mad Again / Whatever Happened To Philip Ford? / Next / Gnomes Of Bromley / Going Slowhere /** Godot Woz Ere.

Dave Pope - Vocals, Guitars, Bass (3, 6, 7, 9, 11), Mandolin (10). Andy Thomson - Bass. PH - Drums, Percussion, Vocals (1, 3, 6, 7, 9). Gemma Gayner - Strings (6, 10), Sings (3, 8). Malcolm Gayner - Vocals (1, 3) Recorded and mixed in Rochester (July 2013) and Faversham (December 2013) by Malcolm Gayner. Sleeve design: Dave Pope [idea: PH; front cover photo: Gemma Gayner]. Produced by Malcolm Gayner & Yellowjack.

BABYLON SQUEAK *Bubblegumboots*

[download / no catalogue number / 2015]

Spoon In Your Sink / The Go-To Guy / Come Clean.

Andy Thomson - guitars, bass, keyboards, drum patterns. PH - vocals, percussion. [However, AT and PH appeared under these aliases: Osama Bin Arnas - voice. Billy O'Knare - guitars, backing voice. Jillian Leatherclouds - keyboards, Wartle. Loder Krudd - bass, backing voice. Johnny Twilite - drums. Nostradamus Pettigrew - felt bass, bamboo thwackery and contraptions.] Artwork: Dave Pope, Karen Birch, Jason Gollop, PH. Produced by Babylon Squeak.

DOUG MURPHY + PAUL HAMILTON
Nope Unintended

[download / no catalogue number / 2016]

IVY / Bluebell Wood / Fly My Plane

DM - guitars, bass, keyboards. PH - vocals, piano strings (2). Sleeve: Dave Pope, Jason Gollop. Produced by Hamilton & Murphy.

THIS LITTLE BADGE *Pass It On*

[USB / 2GB16 / 2016]

Pretend / Meet Me At The Bridge **/ That's All We Need / Babylon Don /** Downtown, Witsend* / Four Chords And A Capo*.

Dave Pope - guitar, vocal. Dave Ritchie Smith - guitar, backing vocal. Hamish Cameron - bass. Adam Colless - drums. Recorded by: Dave Ritchie Smith at Dogdamnit Studio, New Plymouth, NZ. Sleeve concept & design: Dave Pope. Produced by Dave Pope & Dave Ritchie Smith.

RETICENTS *Tough To Trace*

[download / BYTE18 / 2016]

Tough To Trace

Andy Thomson - guitars, keyboards, drum pattern. Dave Toynton - bass. PH - vocal, triangle, keyboard. Sleeve: PH. Produced by Andy Thomson and Si Beex [a.k.a. Simon Beacon].

DOUG MURPHY + PAUL HAMILTON *Car-Toons!*

[download / BYTE17 / 2016]

Sharkey's Machine / Eli Skanko / **Money In The Hat.**

DM - guitars, bass, drum loop (1), mandolin, piano, keyboards. PH - vocals, drums, percussion. Sleeve: PH and Dave Pope. Produced by Hamilton & Murphy.

BABYLON SQUEAK *Hoboho*

[download / BYTE19 / 2016]

Starving In A Limo / Piñata / **Rater Rater** / Hoboho.

Andy Thomson - guitars, bass guitar, keyboards, drum loops, backing vocal (3). PH - vocals, percussion (1,3, 4). Special guests: Si Beex: Defuzzotron (2). Ronnie Burgess: Facticle Gatherizer (3). Artwork: PH. Recorded by Andy. Mixed by Paul. Produced by Hamilton and Thomson.

BABYLON SQUEAK *Nine Minute Holiday*

[download / BYTE20 / 2017]

Postcard From Amnesia / Sunny Ray / Up To You.

Andy Thomson - bass, guitars, keyboards. PH - vocals, percussion, snare drum. Artwork: PH with Dave Pope. Recorded by Andy. Mixed by Paul. Produced by Hamilton and Thomson.

BABYLON SQUEAK *Zen Joints*

[download / BYTE21 / 2017]

Whistles And Bells / Tuppenny Blues / R&R.

Andy Thomson – guitars, bass, keyboards, string arrangement ('Whistles And Bells'), drum and sequencer programming ('R&R'). PH – percussion and voices.Recorded at Toppo Towers and The Hamilslum, May and August 2017. Mastered by Si Beex at the Vulnavium, September 2017.Artwork: PH. Produced by Hamilton and Thomson.

DMPH [*a.k.a.* Doug Murphy & Paul Hamilton] *The Silent Finger*

[download / BYTE22 / 2017]

The Silent Finger (Left Hand) /
The Silent Finger (Right Hand).

DM – guitars, bass, melodica. PH – Drums, percussion, clandestine clatterings, editingzzzzz. Albie Gibbs: Heralding the prophesies of the Pyewhackett. Artwork: PH. Produced by DMPH.

BABYLON SQUEAK *You Don't Get Me*

[download / BYTE23 / 2017]

You Don't Get Me / It's All About You #1 (The Thomsong Templatation) / XXX / It's All About You #2 (The Rammertone Hammerfications).

Andy Thomson – keyboards, bass, guitars, drum patterns. PH – Vocals, percussion, sound effects. Artwork: Christian Brett. Produced by Hamilton and Thomson.

BABYLON SQUEAK *Ch*ppy*

[download / BYTE24 / 2018]

Nobody's Fool / **Dead Leg** / The Enemy Within / **The Last Hello.**

Andy Thomson – keyboards, bass, guitars, drum patterns. PH – Vocals, drums, percussion, sound effects, bass. Phil Harris – harmonica (1, 2). Artwork: PH, tidied up by Dave Pope. Produced by Hamilton and Thomson.

VARIOUS ARTISTS *The Green Book*

[download / BYTE25 / 2019]

Babylon Squeak: **Cottage By The Sea** / This Little Badge: Think Of A Number / DMPH: Slow To Recognise / Yellowjack: **Marwar Junction.**

Andy Thomson (1, 4), Dave Pope (2, 4), Doug Murphy (3), PH (1, 3, 4), Camilla Douglas (1), Sam Johnson (2). Artwork: PH. Produced by PH with substantial input from Dave Pope, Doug Murphy, Si Beex, Jason Gollop and Sam Johnson.

DMPH *Talking About My Genitalia*

[download / BYTE26 / 2020]

Talking About My Genitalia / **Featherstone, Featherstone, Wriothesley** / Rumours Of Peace / Featherstone, Featherstone, Wriothesley (At The Garrick).

DM - Guitars, bass, keyboards, piano, mandolin. PH - Drums, vocals, percussion. Drums recorded by Andy Thomson at Toppo Towers. Artwork: PH. Produced by DMPH.

DMPH *W.A.S.P. In W.E.B.*

[download / BYTE28 / 2020]

W.A.S.P. In W.E.B. / Bubbles.

DM - Guitars, bass, keyboards, piano. PH - Drums, vocals, percussion. Artwork: Dave Pope and PH. Produced by DMPH. (W.A.S.P. In W.E.B co-produced by Si Beex at The Vulnavium.)

DMPH *Instant Coma!*

[download / BYTE29 / 2020]

Look After / **Born To Rest** / Thumbs And Fingers / Bed Rock / Far Fetching.

DM - Guitars, bass, keyboards, piano. PH - Drums, vocals, percussion. Artwork: Dave Pope and PH. Produced by DMPH.

THIS LITTLE BADGE *Marwar Junction*

[download / MINI-BYTE30 / 2021]

Marwar Junction

Performed and produced by Dave Pope and Sam Johnson. Artwork: Dave Pope.

DMPH *Tattoo Removal Service*

[download / MINI-BYTE32 / 2021]

Tattoo Removal Service (Radio Jingle, C90 Cassette) / **Tattoo Removal Service** / Real Got Shit / **Tattoo Removal Service** (TV Advert, VHS Tape)

DM – Guitars, bass, keyboards, piano. PH – Drums, vocals, percussion. Artwork: PH. Produced by DMPH.

STINKY RUBY *Burberry Bouffant*

[download / MINI-BYTE31 / 2021]

Burberry Bouffant / Keep Away From Children, Keep Away From Eyes / &#x27

Track 1: DM – Guitars, bass, vocal, piano, keyboards. PH – Vocal, drums, percussion. Tracks 2 and 3: PH – all instruments and noises. Artwork and production: PH.

DMPH *Punk Is Crap*

[download / MINI-BYTE33 / 2021]

Punk Is Crap / Water Duck Back / Hello, Can I Help You?

DM and PH playing their usual roles. Mixed and mastered by Malcolm Gayner. Artwork: Irene Landa.

DMPH *Breakfast of Champions*

[download / MINI-BYTE34 / 2022]

Breakfast Of Champions.

Artwork: PH with Georgina Micklethwaite. Produced by DMPH.

DMPH *I Can Count Up To Potato*

[download / MINI-BYTE35 / 2022]

I Can Count Up To Potato.

DMPH with Annabelle Gollop (vocal).
Artwork: Dave Pope. Produced by DMPH.

THIS LITTLE BADGE *Rule of Three*

[download / no catalogue number / 2022]

I.C.U. / Think Of A Number / Love Crawls In

Dave Pope with Adam Colless on drums (2) and Sam Johnson on bass and keyboards. Artwork: Dave Pope. Produced by Pope and Johnson.

DMPH ***Bank Of Mum And Dad***

[download / MINI-BYTE37 / 2022]

Bank Of Mum and Dad / Humphrey Go-Kart (I Forgot)

Doug Murphy: Bank Of Mum & Dad - Opening chorale, harp, bass, rhythm guitars, piano, drum patterns, brass, strings, lead guitar. Humphrey Go-Kart - Bass, rhythm and lead guitars, keyboards, brass, backing vocals. Paul Hamilton: Bank Of Mum & Dad - Lead and backing voices, block, tambourine, drum patterns edit, coins, handclaps. Humphrey Go-Kart - Drums, voice. Artwork: PH and Dave Pope. Produced by Paul Hamilton and Doug Murphy.

DMPH ***Do It Myself***

[download / MINI-BYTE39 / 2023]

Do It Myself / New Umbrella / The End Of The World

DM: Bass, guitars, keyboards. PH: Drums, vocal, percussion. Artwork: PH. Produced by DMPH.

DMPH ***We Are Open***

[download / BYTE40 / 2023]

Bank Of Mum and Dad / Tattoo Removal Service / W.A.S.P. In W.E.B. / Look After / Real Got Shit / **Water Duck Back / Humphrey Go-Kart / Breakfast Of Champions / Punk Is Crap**

Compilation of DMPH's favourite songs from 2020–22, most of them remixed. Artwork: PH. Booklet: DMPH. Remastered by DM. Produced by DMPH.

DMPH ***Sultan***

[download / BYTE41 / 2023]

We've Come So Far / **Bill's Brill Grill (Reheated)** / Take A Deep Breath / **The Up Set / SCAB!** / Disturbulence / Pure Mayhem / **Invasion Of BS**

Recorded (mostly) on Saturday 22nd October 2022 at Baker Street West Studio, Haugesund, Norway. DM and PH twanging and banging on their usual instruments. Artwork: PH, Georgina Micklethwaite. Booklet: DMPH. Produced by DMPH.